THE BLACK MUSLIMS

AFRICAN-AMERICAN ACHIEVERS

THE BLACK MUSLIMS

William H. Banks, Jr.

CHELSEA HOUSE PUBLISHERS
Philadelphia

Chelsea House Publishers
Editorial Director Richard Rennert
Production Manager Pamela Loos
Art Director Sara Davis
Picture Editor Judy Hasday

Staff for THE BLACK MUSLIMS
Contributing Editor Therese De Angelis
Senior Editor Jane Shumate
Editorial Assistant Kristine Brennan
Designer Takeshi Takahashi
Picture Researcher Lisa Kirchner
Cover Illustration Robert Gerson

First Printing

1 3 5 7 9 8 6 4 2

Library of Congress Cataloging-in-Publication Data

Banks, William, 1946-
The Black Muslims / William H. Banks, Jr.

128 p.   cm.—(African-American Achievers)
Includes bibliographical references (p. 125) and index.
Summary: A history of the Nation of Islam, from its found-
ing to the present day.

ISBN   0-7910-2593-4
ISBN   0-7910-2594-2 (pbk)

1. Black Muslims—Juvenile literature [1. Black Muslims.]
I. Title. II. Series.
BP221.B36 1996b
297'.87—dc20   96-31055
                                         CIP
                                         AC

Frontispiece: *Headed by the
Fruit of Islam, African-American
men line up near the Washington
Monument for the procession to
the Mall during the Million Man
March.*

On the cover: *Nation of Islam
members gather for their Savior's
Day Convention, held each year
on February 26.*

CONTENTS

AFRICAN-AMERICAN ACHIEVERS

THE BLACK MUSLIMS

1

One Million Strong

THE PREDAWN HOURS of October 16, 1995, were damp and chilly in Washington, D.C. But the weather went almost unnoticed by the thousands of African-American men gathering on the Mall, the grassy stretch of land extending from the steps of the U.S. Capitol Building to the Washington Monument.

Across the country—from Los Angeles to Boston and from Minnesota to Miami—African-American men had heeded a call to action. They arrived by bus and by plane, on foot and in wheelchairs, in business suits and in sweatshirts, carrying briefcases and knapsacks and young children, for the "Million Man March" on the nation's capital. They came to pledge an end to "black-on-black" violence, and to renew their commitment to women, children, family, and church—and to political activism for African Americans.

By mid-morning, the Mall was nearly filled with African-American men, young and old, waving signs and flags. In an ecumenical service punctuated by the beat of African drums, Archbishop George A. Stallings, founder of the Imani African-American Catholic Congregation, delivered the

With the Washington Monument in the background, a participant in the October 16, 1995, Million Man March is carried above the crowd.

opening prayer. "Take the hand of a brother next to you," he began. "We, as proud black men . . . have all sojourned to this gateway of the Promised Land to take ownership and control and lay claim to our own destiny. . . . The opportunities for a brand-new day are here."

The audience listened attentively as more than 50 African-American leaders and dignitaries took their turns speaking at the lectern in front of the Capitol steps. Civil rights leader Jesse Jackson, Betty Shabazz (the widow of Malcolm X), musician Stevie Wonder, civil rights activist Rosa Parks, poet Maya Angelou, and a multitude of religious leaders addressed the throng. "America will benefit and ultimately be grateful for this day," proclaimed Jesse Jackson. "When the rising tide of racial justice and gender equality and family stability lifts the boats stuck at the bottom, all boats benefit."

Late in the afternoon, the crowd began chanting for the man who had called the Million Man March to order: "Farrakhan! Farrakhan! We want Farrakhan!" Finally, the leader of the Nation of Islam stepped to the lectern amid cheers and applause. In a speech over two hours long, Louis Farrakhan exhorted African Americans to "become a totally organized people." He urged them to "become a part of some organization that is working for the uplift of our people. . . . [G]et back to the houses of God. [B]e more like Jesus, more like Muhammad, more like Moses. . . . All we've got to do is go back home and turn our communities into productive places."

Then, in one of the most stirring moments of the event, thousands of African-American men joined hands and recited the pledge on which the march was founded:

> I pledge that from this day forward I will strive to love my brother as I love myself. I . . . will strive to improve myself spiritually, morally, mentally, socially,

politically, and economically for the benefit of myself, my family, and my people. I pledge that I will strive to build businesses, build houses, build hospitals, build factories, and enter into international trade for the good of myself, my family, and my people.

I pledge that from this day forward I will never raise my hand with a knife or gun to beat, cut, shoot any member of my family or any human being except in self-defense. . . . I will never abuse my wife by striking her, disrespecting her, for she is the mother of my children and the producer of my future. . . . I will never engage in the abuse of children. . . . For I will let them grow in peace to be strong men and women for the future of our people. . . .

I pledge that from this day forward I will not poison my body with drugs or that which is destructive to my health and my well-being. . . . I will support black newspapers, black radio, black television. I will support black artists who clean up their act to show respect for their people and respect for the heirs of the human family.

I will do all of this, so help me God.

Many people who had gathered that day could not help recalling another great march on Washington. In 1963, Martin Luther King, Jr., led more than 250,000 people, black and white, to the steps of the Capitol in a demonstration for racial unity and equal rights legislation. Now some of the same men had returned with their sons and grandsons on a spiritual journey that many felt was long overdue. Despite new laws, political gains, and the advances of the civil rights movement of previous decades, African-American boys and men in 1995 often found themselves enmeshed in a cycle of poverty and violence. It had to cease, said Farrakhan, and the only way to break the cycle was for each person to take responsibility for his actions and vow to change.

The Million Man March was not about civil rights. It was a march for economic and political survival in the face of continuing racism. When asked to contribute one dollar toward this cause, the crowd waved a sea of dollar bills in the air. Eight million African Americans were eligible but unregistered to vote, Farrakhan said. Go home and register, he told them. Find eight others and convince them to do the same.

The massive display of African-American brotherhood and commitment was clearly a success. Inspired and bursting with pride, marchers returned home filled with hope, determined to spread the message of the Million Man March to their communities. In the aftermath of this day of prayer, music, and spiritual renewal, drug and alcohol abuse centers across the country reported an increase in volunteers. Neighborhood cleanup crews, voter-registration programs, and homeless shelters sprang up. Church and temple congregations swelled. New job programs and antiviolence campaigns were initiated.

With all the fire and promise it instilled in African Americans, however, the Million Man March—and its leader, Louis Farrakhan—was not without critics. As the head of the Nation of Islam, Farrakhan had frequently railed against the wickedness of whites and their institutions. Indeed, the Nation of Islam itself was a movement traditionally steeped in loathing for the "white devil" who had, thousands of years ago, the Nation held, subjugated and enslaved blacks. Many critics objected to Farrakhan's leading the march because the hatefulness he preached as leader of the Nation of Islam contradicted the affirming message of hope and self-respect that drew so many marchers to Washington.

Jewish Americans in particular were distressed by Farrakhan's presence, for his relationship with them had been exceptionally turbulent. In the years preceding the march, Farrakhan had vehemently attacked Jews, and in 1994 he refused to expel a minister, Khallid Abdul Muhammad, who had delivered a scathing anti-Semitic speech during a

Very small amid monumentality and mixed messages, a young marcher pauses during the Million Man March to read an inscription on the wall of the Lincoln Memorial.

college address. This bigotry was even more disturbing, many felt, in light of historical similarities between African Americans and Jews, both of whom had experienced persecution, alienation, and enslavement; for this reason, many Jews had supported the civil rights movement.

That Farrakhan had characterized the march as a "Day of Atonement," an explicit comparison to Yom Kippur, the Jewish solemn holiday of fasting and prayer, did not help the situation. "Were these words said by someone else," asserted one Jewish leader, "it would be easier to accept them as a positive tribute to Jewish observance."

A great deal of criticism concerned the Nation of Islam's history of belief in black supremacy, which appeared to some detractors simply to mirror the white supremacist view that one race was more intelligent, more civilized—in short, better in every way—than all other races, and therefore should dominate others. Traditional teaching of the Black Muslims (as members of the Nation of Islam are often called) held that blacks were the "Original Men" before whites existed and were destined to rule the earth.

For similar reasons, many detractors objected to Farrakhan's "men only" invitation to Washington. In keeping with Black Muslim thinking that black men are guardians of women—whose place is in the home—Farrakhan had asked black women not to attend the march. Instead, he said, they should stay home, praying and teaching their children about self-esteem and family unity. Was this "segregation" of men and women not itself a form of discrimination?

Other critics of Farrakhan's march feared an outbreak of the violence that had plagued the Nation of Islam in the 1970s, when internal conflicts had exploded into bloodshed, claiming the lives of disillusioned ex-members and their families. The intensity and rage of Black Muslim rhetoric was at times alarming. Would it incite violence in an already troubled crowd?

But the Million Man March was peaceful and reflective. In the days following the event, those who attended it described an overwhelming feeling of unity with their "brothers." Many told stories of encounters with strangers whom they somehow felt they had known for years. A great number of those attending the march said they had been drawn to it not by the separatist philosophy of Louis Farrakhan and the Nation of Islam, but by the opportunity to celebrate what many African Americans had long sought: self-love, respect, and a unified community.

The fact that Farrakhan's divisive words were eclipsed by his concept of a nationwide commit-

ment to the betterment of African-American life should not have surprised most of his critics. After all, African-American improvement and financial self-sufficiency were original tenets of the Nation of Islam's philosophy. The movement's founder, Wallace Fard, established the Nation in 1930 as a group devoted to promoting African-American pride and independence. Its first national leader, Elijah Muhammad, expanded the organization's goals to include black economic autonomy and social responsibility by extending material support to the poor and dispossessed. Later, during the 1950s and 1960s, the Nation of Islam fostered black political awareness by offering its separatist ideology as an alternative to the integration-minded civil rights movement.

The prospect of one million African-American men marching in Washington, D.C., may have made many whites—and many of Farrakhan's critics—uneasy. Yet the Nation of Islam has much more to offer than rage and rhetoric. Indeed, it has a long history of providing solidarity and purpose for blacks who have been jostled to the economic and political edges of American society.

Participants in the March embrace. Many who attended were overwhelmed by the atmosphere of brotherhood among strangers in the largest gathering of African Americans in United States history.

2

"Up, You Mighty Race!"

At the turn of the century, 90 percent of the country's black population lived in the South, predominantly in rural areas. Many endured the harsh poverty shown in this photo of a Georgia sharecropper's family.

BETWEEN 1900 AND 1930, nearly three million African Americans left the South to seek their fortunes in the North, sending the black population of the North soaring by 400 percent. A 1910 census recorded that 90 percent of the nation's black population lived in the South, three-quarters of them in rural areas. Fifty years later, the numbers had reversed—three-quarters of all African Americans lived in northern cities. Although African Americans had been moving north since the time of the Civil War, the largest migration boom occurred around World War I, when nearly a half million rural blacks left the South. Race relations certainly played a part in this mass exodus. But the primary force behind the shift in population was economic.

In the early 1910s, cotton plantations in the South were devastated by a sudden influx of beetles called boll weevils. These cotton-eating insects entered the United States through Mexico and gradually ate their way eastward, ravaging crops throughout the South and drastically reducing the already limited holdings of black tenant farmers. Then, in 1915, hundreds of thousands of blacks were left homeless when flood waters washed over riverbanks in Alabama and Mississippi.

During the same period, World War I stimulated economic growth in the more industrialized North. Factories that manufactured military equipment had to increase their productivity, and unskilled and semiskilled laborers found themselves in great demand. Northern manufacturers even sent industrial agents into the South to search for men to fill the positions left vacant by those who had gone to war. So acute was the shortage of workers that these agents sometimes paid transportation costs for entire families to move north.

In 1917, three years after the onset of World War I, the United States joined Britain, Russia, France, and Italy in the conflict against Germany, Austria-Hungary, and the Ottoman Empire (present-day Turkey and the Middle East). President Woodrow Wilson declared that America had entered the war to "make the world safe for democracy." But many African Americans thought this assertion hypocritical at best: for years, blacks living in the democratic United States had been denied basic human rights.

Nevertheless, African Americans joined the armed forces in great numbers: more than two million registered for the draft, established in 1917; ultimately, 367,000 African Americans entered military service during World War I, and 42,000 saw combat. Though African Americans in the military were often relegated to menial jobs such as unloading ships, cleaning latrines, and digging ditches, those who saw combat performed brilliantly. The all-black New York 369th Infantry Division and the Illinois 371st Infantry regiment, for example, both

Black workers harvest cotton on a southern plantation around 1900. Boll weevil infestation and a devastating flood during the 1910s further impoverished black tenant farmers in the South, leading nearly a half million blacks to migrate north.

earned the prestigious Croix de Guerre, the highest medal awarded by the French government, for their gallantry in battle against the Germans in France, and the United States bestowed the Distinguished Service Cross on 26 members of the 371st.

While the war raged in Europe, the vast migration of African Americans to the North continued. Black intellectuals of the time—such as Robert Abbott, publisher and editor of the *Chicago Defender,* and W. E. B. Du Bois, activist and editor of the *Crisis,* the widely read journal published by the National Association for the Advancement of Colored People (NAACP), the nation's leading antidiscrimination organization—applauded this "moving fever." They proclaimed that it would finally put an end to the South's old order of black oppression and black compliance with racism.

As World War I ended, the urgent call for manpower ceased. Jobs became harder to find as manufacturing slowed and as soldiers returned, ready to rejoin the work force. African Americans who had fought in World War I came home with the hope that their wartime sacrifices would be repaid by gains in civil rights. But job-seeking whites felt threatened by the great number of blacks also looking for work, and white racists in particular believed that military-trained blacks would be too powerful to control. Far from diminishing, racial friction increased after World War I.

By 1917, one year before the war ended, the animosity of white workers toward blacks was already so great that race riots had erupted in both Philadelphia and Chester, Pennsylvania. In July of that same year, the black ghetto of East St. Louis, Illinois, witnessed one of the worst race riots of the century. The violence began when a group of whites drove through East St. Louis, randomly spraying gunfire into black homes. As night fell, some blacks mistook a police car for the Ford driven by the whites and shot at the car. Two policemen were killed. Later that night, whites retaliated. They burned down the homes of the blacks and killed the occupants as they attempted to flee from the burning buildings. At least 39 people were hanged, clubbed, shot, or stabbed to death. A few weeks later, a similar series of hostile events precipitated a riot in Houston, Texas.

By 1919, one year after the end of World War I, racial relations in America had seriously deteriorated. The *Crisis*, the NAACP's journal, printed an article by W. E. B. Du Bois, who urged African Americans to respond to this postwar shift in for-

tunes with militant action: "We return from the slavery of the uniform which the world's madness demanded us to don to the freedom of civil garb," he wrote. "*We return. We return from fighting. We return fighting.* Make way for Democracy!"

But white America had other ideas. Later that year, race riots broke out in about two dozen cities across the United States, including Washington, D.C., Chicago, and Knoxville, Tennessee. More than 60 blacks were lynched, a steady stream of bloodshed that prompted James Weldon Johnson, NAACP field secretary, to refer to the season with the greatest number of riots as "the Red Summer."

African Americans began responding to the threat of violence by organizing themselves. And in the early 1920s, no one was playing a greater role in bringing his people together than Jamaican-born

Members of the all-black 369th Infantry march through New York City upon their return from World War I in 1919. Dubbed the "Hell Fighters" by the Germans, the members of the 369th performed brilliantly during the war but came home to increased racial hatred and violence.

Marcus Garvey. An advocate of racial separatism, he offered a unique vision that captured the imagination of African Americans across the nation.

As a young man, Garvey campaigned, both in his native Jamaica and in Central America, against the brutal treatment of his fellow West Indian workers. When these efforts were unsuccessful, he traveled to London in 1912, hoping to persuade the British government to change its policies toward colonial workers. Garvey was again unable to find a way to alleviate the suffering of the workers. But he had begun to read extensively about black history and eventually discovered Booker T. Washington's autobiography, *Up from Slavery,* an inspiring account of how the author rose from being a janitor to an educator and America's leading black spokesman.

Upon returning to Jamaica in 1914, Garvey founded the Universal Negro Improvement Association (UNIA), an organization intent on promoting black pride. When the UNIA failed to take hold in Jamaica, Garvey shifted its headquarters to Harlem, New York. A great number of African Americans migrating from the South had settled in Harlem, and when Garvey arrived it was one of the largest African-American communities in the country and a thriving black business and cultural center. By 1919, the UNIA had found its supporters, claiming a worldwide membership of two million, with branches in Chicago, Philadelphia, New Orleans, and Los Angeles.

At the heart of Garvey's movement was his desire to see blacks educate themselves so that they could achieve economic independence and political power. He urged them to shed their sense of disillusionment, to take pride in their race, and to free themselves from dependence on white employers and institutions. "Where is the black man's Government?" he would ask. "Where is his King, and his kingdom, his navy, his men of big affairs?" Telling his listeners that he had never seen such things, he would then declare, "I will help to make them."

And so he did. Traveling widely through the United States and Canada, the dynamic Garvey spoke tirelessly about the need for universal solidarity among blacks and about the importance of working to raise oneself out of poverty and oppression. "Up, you mighty race!" he would cry. "You can accomplish what you will!" His words thrilled African Americans who had grown restless and discouraged by racial injustice and economic hardship, and UNIA membership quickly grew.

In 1918, Garvey, a former printer, had begun publishing *Negro World*, a weekly newspaper for the UNIA. Filled with information on events and issues of interest to blacks, the paper was distributed in the United States, Canada, the West Indies, Latin America, Europe, and Africa, with a peak circulation of more than 60,000. Through *Negro World*, many readers gained their first glimpse of black life in other parts of the world.

In late 1919, Garvey invited all UNIA branches and other black organizations around the globe to send delegates to UNIA headquarters in New York for a huge display of black solidarity. On August 1, 1920, the International Convention of the Negro Peoples of the World opened with religious services and a silent march of delegates and UNIA members through Harlem. The convention continued through the month, with speeches, fund-raising events, and rallies. Delegates even set up a model black government and composed a Declaration of Rights of the Negro Peoples of the World, to be presented to all the world's governments.

But the event that drew the most attention was the spectacular parade of August 2. Led by members of the African legions wearing blue and red uniforms and riding on horseback, the parade present-

Ku Klux Klan members emerge from a tunnel in Stone Mountain, Georgia, 1921. The white supremacist organization fed on the fears of Americans who felt threatened by thousands of blacks migrating North and by European immigrants arriving in America in unprecedented numbers.

ed a military show that revealed the untapped power of the African race. Following the riders were 200 Black Cross nurses in long white dresses. Though few had medical training, the group symbolized the UNIA's commitment to aiding the sick and needy members of black communities.

Garvey himself rode in an open car, wearing a uniform with fringed epaulets and carrying a cane in his white-gloved hands. Although he was short in stature, his long-plumed helmet made him easy to single out as the leader of the parade. "The nations of the world are aware that the Negro of yesterday has disappeared," Garvey declared at the close of the convention. "His place has been taken by a new

Negro who stands erect, conscious of his manhood rights and fully determined to preserve them at all costs."

But Garvey was easy to single out in another way. Unlike the nation's more moderate black leaders, such as W. E. B. Du Bois, he strongly opposed integration efforts, favoring black separatism instead. In fact, as time went by, Garvey promoted himself as a Black Moses striving to lead his people back to their African homeland. Though this dream was never realized, black separatist groups kept alive his Back-to-Africa concept for many decades.

Garvey did not only look to promote a euphoric sense of hope among his followers; his organization also produced concrete results. His weekly newspaper, *Negro World*, helped encourage the formation of numerous African-American businesses. He even began his own shipping company, the Black Star Line, an economic venture operated solely by blacks, with the aim to link black commerce worldwide and to transport black Americans to their African homeland.

Despite its initial success, the UNIA soon faltered. In 1922, Garvey shocked many of his followers by forming a pact with the Ku Klux Klan (KKK), a white supremacist organization notorious for its violent attacks against African Americans. Although he never claimed admiration for the Klan, Garvey believed that he and the KKK stood on similar ground on one important issue: both wanted blacks out of the country. Because the Klan wholeheartedly supported racial separatism, Garvey went so far as to say that Klansmen were "better friends of the [black] race" than the integrationist NAACP.

By forming such a strange alliance, Garvey spurred politically moderate African Americans, especially those in the press, to attack the UNIA. He supplied them with even more ammunition when the Black Star Line, whose finances he had mismanaged from the start, collapsed. Matters grew worse for Garvey in 1923, when he was convicted of mail fraud; he had allegedly made illegal use of America's postal service by selling phony stock for his shipping enterprise.

As the Black Star Line sank, the UNIA went down with it. Garvey was sent to a federal penitentiary in Atlanta, Georgia, in 1925, and, after serving almost half of his five-year prison sentence, he was deported to Jamaica. U.S. officials never again allowed him entry into America.

Lacking political and economic power in the early decades of the 20th century, African Americans sought other channels of relief from their difficulties, turning to religious movements for leadership and spiritual guidance. In urban ghettos in particular this tendency often assumed political overtones. Deprived of justice, equality, and an improved standard of living by a white-run society, they sought other organizations like the UNIA, where they could freely participate in business, politics, and social reform. For those interested in forming a black homeland overseas, for example, there was the Peace Movement of Ethiopia, which supported the racist Mississippi senator Theodore G. Bilbo's bill to repatriate black Americans in Africa. The National Movement for the Establishment of the 49th State sought to create a black state within the United States. The Father Divine Peace Missions emerged as another popular movement; led by George Baker, who had assumed the name Father Divine in the early 1900s, the peace missions won legions of followers by providing low-cost or free food to poor African Americans during the Depression.

Garvey's UNIA had been one of the largest and earliest of such groups. But while he was launching the UNIA, another, more religiously oriented black

Marcus Garvey in full military-style dress during the 1920 International Convention of the Negro Peoples of the World in Harlem, New York. One of the earliest and most popular black nationalist movements in America, the Universal Negro Improvement Association (UNIA) appealed to blacks worldwide and inspired similar organizations such as the Moorish Temple of America and the Nation of Islam.

nationalist movement was forming: Noble Drew Ali's Moorish Temple of America. Ali fired the imagination of lower-class African Americans and amassed a large following by claiming that blacks were superior to whites. The white race, he added, was doomed.

According to Ali's followers, the Moorish Temple of America was founded after the North Carolina-born Ali visited Morocco. There the king told him to teach the Moroccan religion, Islam, to African Americans. Ali established his first temple in Newark, New Jersey, in 1915 and urged all African Americans to refer to themselves as Moorish Americans (the Moors having originally lived in present-day Morocco and Algeria). "Christianity is for the European (paleface); Moslemism is for the Asiatic (olive-skinned)," Ali taught his followers. "When each group has its own peculiar religion, there will be peace on earth."

As his teachings spread to the Midwest, Ali issued national identification cards to his followers. These cards bore the symbols of Islam: a star and crescent, an image of clasped hands, and an encircled number seven. The cards also declared that the bearer believed in "all the Divine Prophets, Jesus, Muhammad, Buddha, and Confucius."

Ali derived his version of Islam from a variety of sources: Eastern philosophy, the Quran, and the Bible. He also drew on assorted anecdotes about Jesus Christ and, as the UNIA leader gained more and more attention, about Marcus Garvey. Followers of the Moorish Temple of America were forbidden to go to movies and dance halls and were not supposed to use cosmetics, hair straighteners, tobacco, or alcohol—all products believed to be unclean or unhealthful. Ali's teachings emphasized a healthy diet and natural herbal remedies, and they were paired with the selling of charms, relics, magical potions (a sample recipe was billed as Old Moorish Herb Tea for Human Ailments), and pictures that were associated with blacks of supposedly Islamic origin.

To make themselves appear more like their African counterparts, Ali's male followers donned red fezzes and grew beards. Accompanying this new look was an open contempt for police and for whites, whom the Moorish Americans called Europeans.

By the mid-1920s, the Moorish Temple of America had attracted droves of newcomers, many of whom had previously been Garveyites. But in

1929, Noble Drew Ali was implicated in the murder of the philanthropist Julius Rosenwald, and his movement fell apart. He died soon after from what were said to be mysterious causes.

At about the same time, the crash of the New York Stock Exchange in October of 1929 ravaged the entire nation, marking the beginning of an economic depression that lasted well into World War II. Millions of unskilled laborers lost their jobs, and skilled laborers who managed to keep working suffered a drastic drop in income. Soup kitchens were set up to offer free meals to the unemployed, and the government established federal relief funds to be distributed to the needy across the country. During the Great Depression, as this period came to be known, between one quarter and one third of the country's work force was unemployed.

African Americans suffered even more severely during this period: black unemployment soared to

When the New York Stock Exchange crashed in 1929, millions of unskilled laborers lost their jobs and were forced to receive federal unemployment relief. These desperate conditions often led to unrest. Here, New York City police rope in a crowd after quelling a riot among men waiting in a relief line.

about 50 percent nationwide, and in some large cities it reached even higher rates—65 percent in Atlanta, Georgia, and 80 percent in Norfolk, Virginia. African-American workers were usually the first to be let go; nearly half of those who lost their jobs had been domestic servants and were replaced by white workers, many of whom had previously considered such work too menial.

All over the country, lines of needy people formed outside local Department of Welfare buildings seeking federal relief money. Even when working, African Americans on the whole earned less than white workers. During the Depression, local relief efforts often did not reach as many blacks as whites, and in the South, unemployed blacks received only about 60 percent of what whites received each month.

Though by this time the UNIA and the Moorish Temple of America had died out, African Americans increasingly sought solace in black-founded religious and political organizations. Among the more radical movements to form during these years was the Lost-Found Nation of Islam. During the summer of 1930, a small, earnest, light-skinned man who usually went by the name of Wallace Fard arrived in Detroit. Acting as a door-to-door peddler, he quickly managed to make himself welcome in the homes of Detroit's black neighborhoods, especially in the misnamed Paradise Valley. Fard told his prospective customers that the silk items he was selling had been worn by blacks in their ancestral homeland across the Atlantic.

A short time later, after he had gained their confidence, Fard began holding meetings devoted to a topic other than business. Fard claimed to be a prophet from Arabia who had come to the United States to help black Americans discover their dual African and Islamic heritages. He told his listeners that they, not whites, were the chosen people. The first humans to walk the earth had been black, he said, "long before the white man stood up on his hind legs and crept out of the caves of Europe."

The white man, Fard continued, was the devil himself. The embodiment of evil, whites had enslaved blacks and robbed them of their African names, giving them Christian names instead. To reclaim their rightful place in the world, blacks should reject the surname given by their slave-holders and adopt an Islamic name or use an X or combination of X's and other letters to symbolize a spiritual rebirth. With help from Fard and the Nation of Islam, he told them, blacks would learn to respect their heritage, gain a sense of discipline, and work to overcome their white oppressors.

Fard offered hope to dispossessed and dispirited African Americans. Many were drawn to his mes-sage of self-sufficiency and renewal, and within three years of his arrival in Detroit he had recruited and organized 8,000 followers. By 1934, the Nation of Islam had become a cohesive community that included an elementary school for Muslim children, training classes for women on how to be proper wives and mothers, and a private security force.

One of Fard's most zealous listeners was a young man named Elijah Poole, who, like thousands of African Americans, had traveled North during the Great Migration. Elijah, his wife, Clara, and their young son, Emmanuel, had settled in Detroit in 1923 in a house that lacked many bare essentials, including a toilet. During the 1920s, the house would hold three more Poole children: Ethel, Nathaniel, and Lotte. Clara would help support the family by working as a domestic.

Elijah Poole was among the many who lost their jobs and stood in relief lines after the economic crash of 1929. Like many others, he and his family faced extremely lean times. The Pooles often sub-sisted on such meals as boiled chicken feet and discarded vegetables that the children would salvage from garbage cans behind grocery stores. Coal for the kitchen stove, which was used to heat the house, was collected from the beds along the railroad tracks. Nothing of even the slightest use was thrown away. The four Poole children wore hand-me-downs given to Clara by the people for whom she cleaned, washed, and ironed.

With no alternative, Poole remained on relief until 1931. Every morning, he left home before dawn to join the lines of thousands of unemployed people that formed in front of the gates of local manufacturing plants. He often waited there all morning, hoping to be hired for a day's work, only to return home empty-handed to his four children.

Soon after his move to Detroit, Elijah had begun to believe that he was destined for religious work. He had grown up with his 12 brothers and sisters listening to the fiery sermons of his father, Wali Poole, a sharecropper and Baptist minister, in a small town in Georgia. But he believed that Christianity could provide neither spiritual nor physical salvation—it would not release African Americans from racial oppression, as many of them seemed to expect. He later told his mother, "[I]t seemed that there was something warning me that I should be a better man, and I should . . . teach a religion or preach . . . [but I could not] . . . preach the Christian religion. . . . something [was] warning me that this is not right."

In his search for spiritual and material relief, Elijah Poole was drawn to the Nation of Islam in 1930. His father wrote to him and urged him to go hear the preaching of Abdul Muhammad, who had been a member of the Moorish Temple of America and had converted to the Nation of Islam.

Elijah was impressed by what Abdul Muhammad had to say, and when he returned to hear Wallace Fard himself, he was convinced that Fard spoke the truth about the plight of blacks in America. Finally, he had found the path for his own ministry.

The impoverished Poole would ultimately find work in Detroit, but of a very different nature than what he sought in job lines: he would become the leader of the Nation of Islam.

3

A Nation Within a Nation

WALLACE FARD'S TEACHINGS varied significantly from those of traditional Islam, which promotes brotherhood among people of all races. His religious movement, in fact, had much more in common with Marcus Garvey's black nationalism and Noble Drew Ali's Moorish Temple of America. As a result, he attracted to the Nation of Islam many of the same people who had been drawn to Garvey and Ali. Fard's "lost sheep" subsequently became known as Black Muslims.

The notion of a black separatist state struck a deep chord in Poole, who had been an ardent Garveyite and was greatly discouraged by the UNIA's collapse. He began regularly attending Fard's seminars, which were usually held in a Detroit tenement basement.

Poole's first encounter with Fard in the fall of 1931 was a turning point in the development of the Nation of Islam. Poole later said of Fard, "I recognized him to be God in person, and that is what he said he was, but he forbade me to tell anyone else. I was a student of the Bible. I recognized him to be the person the Bible predicted would come two thousand years after Jesus' death. It came to me the

Elijah Muhammad (center, with book) after becoming chief minister of the Nation of Islam in 1933. A follower of Marcus Garvey, Muhammad was disappointed by the demise of Garvey's UNIA and found in Wallace Fard a "savior" for the black race.

first time I laid eyes on him." Although Fard had not previously publicized himself as Allah, or a divine being, he quickly adopted the role Poole ascribed to him, presenting himself at the next meeting as "the Jesus" for whom his followers had been waiting.

One evening, Elijah Poole persuaded his wife, Clara, to attend one of Fard's lectures, while he stayed home with the children. During his talk that evening, Fard asked whether anyone knew "the little man who lives in Hamtramck" (the section of Detroit where the Pooles lived). "Yes," answered Clara, "he is my husband." Fard told Clara that Elijah should "go ahead and teach Islam" with Fard's full support.

Inspired by the leader's faith in him and certain that Fard was a holy man, Poole became one of his first converts. He was soon given an Islamic name, Elijah Muhammad, and became Fard's chief lieutenant, helping him to rouse support for the Nation of Islam by offering hope to African Americans.

As the Nation grew over the next two years, Fard chose to remain a man of mystery. He went by several names, among them Wali Farrad, Professor Ford, Farrad Mohammed, F. Mohammed Ali, and occasionally Allah. Little is known about his early life, and much of the information that does exist is contradictory. For his followers, his enigmatic character added to his air of divinity.

Though Fard may have embellished or exaggerated the details of his life, the origins of his teachings were not quite so mysterious. The Nation drew its principles not only from the Quran but also from the Bible, books about Freemasonry, and the philosophy of Joseph F. ("Judge") Rutherford, the leader of the Jehovah's Witnesses (a religious movement that focuses on the second coming of Christ). Fard himself wrote esoteric manuals defining his religious movement: *The Secret Ritual for the Nation of Islam* and *Teaching for the Lost-Found Nation of Islam in a Mathematical Way*. The latter publication, a sort of catechism (instruction in question-and-answer format) filled with obscure symbolism, was transmitted orally to newly enlisted Black Muslims; its information was forbidden to whites.

Although the Nation's teachings drew upon other religions, its story of creation is unique. According to Fard, the world was initially ruled by members of a black race, who were the original inhabitants of an enormous planet. Theirs was a highly advanced civilization, centered in the city of Mecca, and their scientists formed mountains and seas and covered the land with animals. When an explosion divided the planet into the earth and the moon, the surviving "original men," as they were called, settled in the fertile Nile Valley and became known as the Tribe of Shabazz. They lived in peace for 6,000 years, until evil entered the world in the form of a mad scientist named Yacub.

Full of pride, Yacub set out to gain absolute power over his people. Having discovered the principles of magnetism—that unlike forces attract each other and like forces repel—he applied this concept to society, concluding that, to establish control over all people, he must create a race of "unlike men." He set about teaching his ideas to others and began to draw followers. But having broken the laws of Islam by doing this, Yacub and his disciples were deported from Mecca to the island of Pelan (believed to be near present-day Greece).

His heart set on vengeance, Yacub applied his knowledge of genetics to create from his followers over the next 600 years a race of immoral men, the "white devils." They returned to Mecca to avenge themselves, causing disruption and endless trouble for the original black inhabitants. Finally, they were rounded up and banished to Europe.

The whites lived in Europe for thousands of

Wallace Fard as photographed on May 26, 1933, by the Detroit police department. Under suspicion for operating a "voodoo cult," Fard was arrested three times before police ordered him to leave Detroit.

years, gaining dominion over the entire world. Evil by nature, they committed innumerable atrocities, including taking blacks into slavery. They transported millions of blacks from Africa to the Americas in slave ships, stripping them of their language and cultural heritage and brainwashing them into believing that whites were their superiors. It was time, said Fard, for the 6,000-year rule of the "blue-eyed devils" to end.

Before this could take place, however, blacks needed to become aware of their history and their destiny. Fard told his followers that he was the *Mahdi,* the almighty being, both person and God, that would lead them back to their original state of grace.

To outsiders, especially those who had been raised as Christians, Fard's religious doctrines seemed extreme and his proclamation of divine authority sacrilegious. Yet his supporters believed in him and in his message of racial pride. To the Black Muslims, the history of mankind according to Fard was no less believable than the story of creation told in the Bible.

But Fard was not merely a storyteller. One of the reasons he attracted so many followers was that he gave direction to their lives. Years later, in his book, *Message to the Blackman in America,* Elijah Muhammad would set down all of Fard's original teachings, so that new members would have a "guidebook" for the rituals and moral code of the Nation of Islam. Black Muslims still follow these teachings.

In order to return to their previous state of perfection, Fard taught, blacks must cleanse their bodies by adhering to a special diet. Traditional foods of southern blacks, such as cornbread, black-eyed peas, chitlins, and pork, are considered unhealthful and are part of a "slave diet"; these foods are to be avoided. Tobacco, alcohol, drugs, and gambling are forbidden. Members of the Nation are required to dress

neatly and be well spoken and respectful of others, especially of other Muslims, at all times.

The daily life of a Black Muslim centers around prayer. According to Elijah Muhammad's directives in *Message to the Blackman in America,* each member, beginning at age seven, is expected to perform five prayer services each day: before sunrise, at noon, in the afternoon, at twilight, and after sunset. Every prayer service consists of two parts, the first to be recited in private, and the other to be performed "in congregation, preferably in a Mosque." To cleanse oneself "in and out," the Black Muslim precedes the first prayer of the day with a ritual washing of "hands and all exposed parts" of the body, which includes rinsing one's mouth. Then he twice proclaims, "Allah is the greatest," and continues by reciting two times, "I bear witness that none deserves to be worshiped besides Allah" and "Muhammad is his last apostle," before beginning the first prayer. "Surely I have turned myself to Thee being upright to Him who originated the heavens and the earth," he begins, and goes on:

> O Allah! I seek Thy refuge from anxiety and grief and
> I seek Thy refuge from lack of strength and laziness

> . . . from cowardice and niggardliness . . . from being overpowered by debt and the oppression of men. O Allah! . . . keep me away from what is prohibited and . . . make me free from want of what is besides Thee.

In imitation of orthodox Islam, Elijah Muhammad requires that these "spiritual refreshments" be recited "standing erect with face towards the east [the Holy City of Mecca] with hands raised.

The family is an essential institution for Nation of Islam members. Believing that they are the Chosen People, the Black Muslims exalt and honor women and children for their role in continuing the race. Yet women are thought to be particularly susceptible to the influences of the devil, just as the Biblical Eve was, and are to be protected but not trusted. "The woman is man's field to produce his nation," Elijah Muhammad wrote. He continued:

> If [man] does not keep the enemy out of his field, he won't produce a good nation. If we love our vegetable crops we will go out and turn up the leaves . . . and look carefully for worms that are eating and destroying the vegetables. We will kill that worm—right? . . . We will even kill one another if we find the other one out there trying to steal that crop.
>
> Is not your woman more valuable than that crop of corn, that crop of cotton, that crop of cabbage, potatoes, beans, tomatoes? . . . [W]e cannot return to our land until we have a thorough knowledge of our own selves. This first step is the control and protection of our own women. There is no nation on earth that has less respect for and as little control of their woman as we so-called Negroes here in America.

For similar reasons, divorce has always been frowned upon by Black Muslims because it divides blacks. Likewise, adultery is an especially serious offense, punishable by expulsion. And interracial marriages are expressly forbidden: "Our women have been and are still being used by the devil white race, ever since we were first brought here to these States as slaves," Elijah wrote. Just as whites do not want intermarriage and would "kill you to protect their women," so Black Muslim men are urged to "guard" black women from white men.

Emphasizing self-sufficiency as the key to independence from the white man, the Nation established a temple in Detroit (Temple Number One) and set up programs to educate Black Muslims and to help them form their own businesses within the black community. It founded the University of Islam, an elementary school that also provided education for parents, and the Muslim Girls' Training Class to teach young women the principles of home economics and proper social behavior. And Fard organized the Fruit of Islam, a highly disciplined corps of men who were instructed in religious doctrine and self-defense.

Like the organizations of Marcus Garvey and Noble Drew Ali, however, the Nation's reclusiveness attracted controversy—and the attention of the police—almost from the start. In the racially tense atmosphere of Detroit, rumors arose that the Nation was a cult practicing human sacrifice. Fard was twice arrested for allegedly encouraging such sacrifices, and in the spring of 1933, after his third arrest, Fard was ordered to leave town. He went to Chicago, where Elijah Muhammad had established the Nation's Temple Number Two, but he was immediately arrested and jailed by authorities. From jail, Fard summoned Muhammad and appointed him chief official in his absence, responsible for the Nation's administrative affairs and minister of Temple Number One in Detroit.

No sooner had Muhammad assumed leadership than trouble arose between the Detroit police and the Nation. Black Muslims were allegedly surrounding public schools and telling black children to leave them and to study instead at the University of Islam. When the Michigan State Board of Education notified the authorities that the Nation was

Black Muslim women, most wearing the required long dresses and veils, await the trial of Elijah Muhammad in Chicago in 1942. When Muhammad was arrested for draft avoidance and sedition, his wife, Clara, and other Black Muslim women assumed daily operation of the organization.

running an unaccredited school, the police responded by arresting the teachers at the university.

Muhammad immediately went to the jail where the teachers were being held and offered himself up for arrest. He was charged with contributing to the delinquency of minors. Upon hearing that he had been taken into custody, 700 unarmed Black Muslims marched to police headquarters in protest and were greeted by billy club-wielding police who forced them to disperse. When the authorities offered to drop the charges on the condition that all Black Muslim children be enrolled in public school within six months, Muhammad refused and moved the Nation's headquarters to Chicago.

Shortly after this episode, around June 1934, Fard disappeared from the public—as mysteriously, it seems, as he had arrived. Many of his people believed that he had returned to Mecca (the holiest city of Islam) to ready himself for the end of the world. Other members of the Nation claimed that he had been killed by the police. Muhammad claimed that Fard had been deported, although critics of the Black Muslim movement observed that Fard's disappearance and Muhammad's subsequent rise to power were more than coincidental.

Fard's disappearance was a blow to the Nation; internal conflicts that had already existed among members worsened with the loss of the group's spiritual center, and this infighting threatened to destroy the organization. At odds with some of the movement's factions, Muhammad established a separate branch of the Nation: the Temple People, who were part of a sect called the Allah Temple of Islam. When word reached Muhammad that certain members of the rival factions were angered by his actions, he fled Chicago—in fear for his life, he would later say—leaving his wife, Clara, and their five children behind, where he believed they would remain safe.

Muhammad spent the next seven years in hiding, traveling across the country under assumed names. Nevertheless, he quietly continued to preach the precepts of the Temple of Islam whenever possible, claiming that the voice of Fard directed him to spread his message. Thus, although much of the organization's early tenets originated with Wallace Fard, Elijah Muhammad was most responsible for developing and spreading the precepts and practices that shaped the Nation of Islam.

Wherever he traveled, Muhammad saw African Americans in misery. What kind of God, he would ask his listeners, would treat his people with such contempt? The answer: a white man's God. "Christianity," Muhammad said, "is one of the most perfect black-slave making religions on our planet. It has completely killed the so-called Negroes' mentality." His god, Muhammad told his disciples, was a god of peace and righteousness who would restore blacks to their original state at the end of the world.

All of Muhammad's teachings were directed at preparing blacks for the end of the world, or the apocalypse. On Judgment Day, he said, the great holy war between Allah and the devil would destroy the world, leaving only a select few, the chosen people. Those who worshiped Allah would become fearless and receive divine protection from the evil white devils.

Although Muhammad condemned Christianity as a "white man's religion," many of the original teachings of the Nation of Islam were closely linked to the Bible. Because Wallace Fard, Elijah Muhammad, and their early followers were extremely familiar with the myths and revelations of the Bible, these tales often appeared—with notable changes—in the early prophecies of the movement. For example, in Muhammad's *The Message to the Blackman in America*, he identifies the beast named in the biblical book of Revelation as the white race. The woman about to give birth in chapter 12 of Revelation is said to represent the last Apostle of God, Elijah Muhammad, and her child symbolizes the entire black race that has yet to be "delivered." The serpent who tempted Eve in the Book of Genesis appears again in Revelation as the snake waiting to swallow up the "child" being born—the black race. "The Bible is their graveyard," he would say of blacks, "and they must awaken from it."

While Muhammad traveled, his wife, Clara, directed the Temple's development in Chicago. Now greatly reduced in size, the new group had much difficulty finding a permanent gathering place and started out by meeting in private homes. After Muhammad returned to Chicago to assume leadership once more, the Allah Temple of Islam prospered, eventually surpassing in size the original— and by now defunct—Nation of Islam, whose name it assumed. Soon the members moved to rented

halls in the city's South Side ghetto. These meeting places became known as the Temples of Islam.

Muhammad was not in Chicago for long when a conflict of a different sort than the apocalypse he was predicting took place: in December 1941, the United States entered World War II. Maintaining that Black Muslims were forbidden to bear arms or to perform acts of violence unless directed by Allah, Muhammad refused to register for the military draft. The following May, the Federal Bureau of Investigation (FBI) arrested and imprisoned him, along with 11 other black leaders, for draft avoidance and sedition (encouraging others to break the law). In all, over 100 Black Muslims, including two of Muhammad's sons, were arrested.

A handcuffed Muhammad is led to jail by a federal marshal after being arrested in 1942. Claiming the charges were "cooked up" by whites, Muhammad declared, "The devils do not respect anyone's peace."

Muhammad was sentenced to five years in the Federal Correctional Institution at Milan, Michigan. "The devil cooked up the charges," he later declared, adding that he had been "tried and imprisoned for teaching my people the truth about themselves."

More trouble followed. Because they opposed the draft, and because it was believed that a Japanese group had attempted to infiltrate their organization some years earlier, the Black Muslims were suspected of siding with Japan, one of America's enemies in the war. The FBI put the Chicago temple under surveillance, and a subsequent raid by FBI agents yielded a cache of weapons, which led to additional arrests. "It should now be clear," Muhammad said, "that the attacks made upon us by the brutal American police forces with FBI harassment and persecution, that Allah has manifested the white race of America to be nothing but a race of devils."

While Muhammad and the others served prison sentences, the burden of keeping the Nation going fell on the shoulders of the Black Muslim women. They collected iron, paper, and other items and sold them to help keep the Nation afloat financially. Muhammad's wife, now known as Sister Clara, became especially active in running Chicago's Temple Number Two. She corresponded regularly with her husband and visited him in prison. Through her efforts, Muhammad was able to maintain contact with his organization.

In 1943, after six months in prison, Muhammad and other Black Muslims, always properly behaved, managed to convince the authorities that they were sincere in their religious practices. Consequently, their special requirements—dietary restrictions and prayer time, among others—were accommodated. Showing the depth of their religious commitment had yet another effect: prison authorities began entrusting Black Muslims with important tasks.

Muhammad often used depictions of the American flag and a cross, displayed near the picture of a lynching victim, to teach his followers about the creation of man and the history of blacks. Many of the evils visited on the black race in America, Muhammad would preach, could be attributed to the country's unjust political system and to the Christian precept of "turning the other cheek."

Muhammad, who won the respect of inmates and guards alike, was made an orderly of the guards' quarters.

Every evening, in addition to teaching fellow inmates English, history, and numerology (the study of the hidden significance of numbers), Muhammad would discuss the creation of man, as revealed by Wallace Fard, and give an account of the African American man's traumatic loss of his identity and culture. Muhammad traced for his listeners the history of the Black Muslims, from their peaceful existence in Arabia to their lives as slaves in the United States. By providing the inmates with a link to the past, he hoped to give them a sense of pride. Like Marcus Garvey, he wanted his followers to think of themselves as belonging to a unified group.

Muhammad sometimes highlighted his lessons by drawing on a blackboard. One of his most powerful sketches depicted a faceless lynching victim under an American flag; on the other side of the board he would draw the Islamic emblems of a star and crescent. Underneath these images, he would write, "Freedom or Death?" Muhammad would then describe a scene of racial violence he had witnessed as a child in rural Georgia.

Having taken a forbidden shortcut through the woods to his father's tenant farm, young Elijah had come upon a group of white men trailing a black man at the end of a rope, as though he were a horse or mule. They kicked and insulted him unceasingly, even when he tripped and fell. When they reached a sturdy tree, one of the white men untied the rope around the black man's wrists and threw it over a branch. He formed the other end into a noose and slipped it around the black man's neck. The group then hoisted the victim, spluttering and choking, from the ground.

It took only minutes. After the lynchers were sure the man was dead, they passed a bottle among themselves and looked up at his body, admiring their handiwork. Then, as though they had just concluded a day's work, they strolled away, leaving the black man swinging from the tree.

This horrific scene would never leave Elijah's memory. Instead, as he told his fellow prison inmates, it haunted him as a vivid reminder of the brutal treatment that African Americans, especially those in the South, often suffered.

Muhammad was careful to include in his teachings his apocalyptic message about the impending destruction of the earth. He taught that Allah, in the form of Wallace Fard, had told him precisely how the end of the world would occur. He described in great detail an enormous wheel, called the Mother of Planes, which hovered over the earth (much like a similar figure in the Bible's book of Ezekiel). On Judgment Day, the wheel would destroy the earth in a "battle in the sky" by emitting fire and poison gas. "This is only one of the things in store for the white man's evil world," he said. "This is to warn you and me to fly to our own God and people."

But there would be advance warning of this catastrophe, which he called the Fall of America. The Mother of Planes would first drop pamphlets written in Arabic and English, and then a siren in the sky would warn that the end was approaching. Exactly 144,000 blacks would be spared, and they, in turn, would usher in a new era of black dominion.

Muhammad maintained that this cataclysmic event would occur before the year 2000—more specifically, around or before 1970. In the meantime, he said, the only way for blacks to be saved was for them to follow the teachings of Allah and to prepare for Judgment Day. "We the black people of the earth," he counseled, "are number one owners of it, the best of all human beings. You are the Most Powerful, the Most Beautiful, and the Wisest."

In 1946, Muhammad was released from prison. He returned immediately to Chicago, where he resumed his role as leader of the Nation. The many years that he had spent in flight and in prison showed other Black Muslims how devoted he was to their cause, and cemented his claim to leadership over the growing organization, whose rivals had long since disintegrated.

Muhammad began comparing himself to the persecuted prophets of the Bible and the Quran. Like Muhammad, the founder and last prophet of Allah in traditional Islam, Elijah Muhammad became known as the last Messenger of Wallace Fard, sent to awaken African Americans to their original status as rulers of the earth. Now that blacks were aware of their true heritage, they could begin to prepare for the Fall of America and the promised return to their original state of grace.

NEGRO ENTERPRISE
JAMES P. ROBERTS
PRES.

heingo

RA DRY

er Beer

We Have
Schaefer
AND OTHER GOOD BEERS
ON ICE

CANADA DRY
CREAM SODA

CANA
CREAM S

Beer and Ale

25¢
Per Quart

WINNER

4

"Build Black, Buy Black"

During the 1940s, Muhammad concentrated the Nation of Islam's resources on establishing economic independence for African Americans. Urging members to "build black, buy black," Muhammad—beginning in 1947 with a combined grocery, bakery, and restaurant—expanded the Nation's business enterprises to include factories, farms, real estate, and machine service shops. By the mid-1950s, Black Muslim assets were estimated at $10 million.

WHILE SERVING TIME in prison, Elijah Muhammad realized that most African American churches and civil rights organizations lacked well-developed social programs for the poor. After he was released from prison in 1946, he was determined to apply the Nation's philosophy of black pride and solidarity to projects for helping the needy and giving them direction. Through the Nation, he offered food and work to the outcast and the unemployed— particularly to juvenile delinquents, prostitutes, and former convicts—and helped drug addicts overcome their dependence on narcotics. In providing society's dispossessed with spiritual guidance, the Nation helped to improve thousands of lives. And the movement often gained new converts as a result. Membership rose from a few thousand in the 1940s to tens of thousands over the next decade and a half.

In accordance with strict rules, members of the Nation of Islam were prohibited from spending money on alcohol, tobacco, gambling, or other vices. They were expected to save enough in this way to contribute at least 10 percent of their income to the movement. A great portion of their remaining income, according to Muhammad, should be put toward helping other African Americans.

The results of this program were remarkable. A survey of Black Muslims in Detroit during the Great Depression revealed that during the early 1930s most were on public welfare or received some other form of financial assistance. By the mid-1940s, however, the majority of Black Muslims held jobs and were better off financially than other African Americans. Many of them had moved from inner-city ghetto areas, though they continued to hold meetings there. This upward mobility of Black Muslims was due in part to the revival of the American economy, but it also demonstrated the fruits of their disciplined way of life.

Not surprisingly, the Nation's economic programs expanded as membership increased. Declaring that whites had convinced blacks to settle for menial jobs rather than aspire to become self-sufficient, Muhammad stressed the need to "[b]uild black, buy black." In the summer of 1947, he opened a combined grocery, bakery, and restaurant, one of the first businesses to realize Wallace Fard's dream of financial independence for blacks.

One of the people who was drawn to the Nation's teachings during these years of expansion was Malcolm Little, a black inmate at Norfolk State Prison in Massachusetts. Little's childhood had been filled with racial violence. His family had been driven out of Omaha, Nebraska, by the Ku Klux Klan, and settled in East Lansing shortly after Malcolm's birth. In 1929, when Malcolm was four years old, another white hate group known as the Black Legionnaires set fire to the Littles' house. "I remember being snatched awake into a frightening confusion of pistol shots and shouting and smoke and flames," he recalled years later. "Our home was burning down around us. . . . The white police and firemen came and stood around watching as the house burned down to the ground."

Roxbury, Massachusetts, where Malcolm Little spent his teenage years. He would return to Roxbury in 1953 as Malcolm X—a Nation of Islam minister ready to establish his first temple.

Like Elijah Muhammad, Malcolm Little's father, Earl, was strongly attracted to Marcus Garvey's separatist UNIA. He was president of a branch of the organization, while Malcolm's mother, Louise, worked for it as a reporter. A fearless activist, Earl Little was frequently the target of harassment and threats by white supremacists. Malcolm often accompanied his father to UNIA meetings, where Marcus Garvey's words, adopted as the organization's anthem, thrilled and inspired the young boy: "Up, you mighty race! You can accomplish what you will!"

One day in 1931, hours after Earl Little had left his house, his body was found on a section of trolley tracks downtown. Little's family and friends, including Malcolm, were certain that he had been a victim of white supremacists, but his slayers were never found.

Whether or not Earl Little was murdered, his death had a profound effect on the economic and emotional well-being of his family. His wife, left to provide for eight children during the Depression years, was eventually forced to accept public relief. Although the family was determined to stay together, welfare investigators repeatedly visited the Little

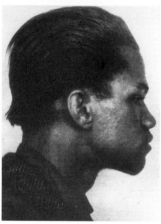

Malcolm Little had had many run-ins with the law before his arrest for robbery in 1945. A wildly angry man, Malcolm earned the nickname "Satan" for his violent outbursts and ferocious behavior in prison.

home in an effort to break it up.

Finally, the pressures of maintaining the household in the face of these difficulties were too great for Louise Little. In 1937, when Malcolm was 12, authorities committed Louise to a mental institution, and Malcolm and his brothers and sisters became wards of the state. The younger six children, including Malcolm, were placed in several foster homes. Years later, filled with anguish and bitterness, Malcolm would refer to the forced separation of his family as "legal, modern slavery—however kindly intentioned."

Angry and alienated, Malcolm had already clashed with the law more than once by the time he was 11 years old. He was sent to a juvenile detention center at age 13, despite his great intellectual promise in school.

In 1939, having heard of the fate of her father's second family, Malcolm's half-sister Ella, a child from Earl Little's first marriage, offered her assistance to Malcolm and his siblings. Ella was especially drawn to Malcolm, and in 1940 she invited him to live with her in Boston.

Though Ella lived in a wealthy section of Roxbury, one of Boston's predominantly black neighborhoods, the excitement and danger of the city's black ghettos were powerful lures to the 15-year-old. At first, Malcolm took a job as a shoe shiner and later as a soda-fountain clerk. But he eventually began selling and using drugs, and he gave up his job because it conflicted with his desire to be on the streets of Roxbury at night, drinking, dancing, and gambling.

In December 1941, eager to see the leading center of African-American culture and politics, Malcolm settled in a boardinghouse in Harlem and took a job waiting tables in a nightclub. There, he was drawn into the New York underworld of thievery, drug dealing, and prostitution.

When he was arrested for robbery and sentenced

to jail in 1945 at age 20, Malcolm was a wildly angry, antisocial young man. He was perversely proud of being an outcast and relished the nickname of "Satan" that he earned from his fellow inmates at Boston's Charlestown State Prison.

In prison, Malcolm stubbornly resisted all efforts to improve his attitude. His rebellious, hostile behavior often landed him in solitary confinement, but he liked being alone and would pace his cell, railing against everyone and everything in savage, antireligious outbursts. His relatives tried to help him adjust, writing letters and visiting whenever possible, but to no avail.

His first step toward reform came when he met an older prisoner named Bimbi. A professional burglar and veteran of many prisons, Bimbi had used his time in jail to broaden his mind by studying such subjects as grammar, history, and philosophy. He was greatly admired by Charlestown's prisoners for his knowledge and for the eloquence with which he defended his opinions.

Malcolm and Bimbi worked together in the prison workshop. During a short break from work one day, Malcolm delivered a scalding attack on religion. Bimbi demolished Malcolm's argument without raising his voice or using the profanity that so appealed to Malcolm. Although Bimbi did not change the young inmate's views, he demonstrated how an intelligent and masterful speaker could take control of an audience. "He was the first man I had ever seen command total respect . . . with his words," said Malcolm.

Eventually, Malcolm stopped resisting efforts to better himself. He enrolled in educational correspondence courses and began studying in the prison library. As he educated himself, he began to see his own experiences from a broader perspective—as a black youth struggling to find a place in American society. Slowly, he transformed himself from a self-centered hustler into a socially conscious black activist.

Malcolm's brothers Philbert and Reginald and his sister Hilda had been writing to him for some time about their conversion to what they called the "natural religion for the black man," the Nation of Islam. Their brother had always responded to their letters with crude, sarcastic insults. But by the time Malcolm was transferred to Norfolk Prison in Massachusetts in 1948, he was ready to listen. A letter from Reginald ended with a strange proposition. "Don't eat any pork, and don't smoke any more cigarettes. I'll show you how to get out of prison."

Intrigued by his brother's words, Malcolm followed his instructions and waited for the solution to this riddle. As time went on, Reginald taught him more and more about the Nation of Islam, and Malcolm was deeply moved by the teachings of Elijah Muhammad. "You don't even know who you are," Reginald wrote. "[T]he white devil has hidden it from you, that you are a race of people of ancient civilizations, and riches in gold and kings. . . . You have been cut off by the devil white man from all true knowledge of your own kind."

For Malcolm, who had had little direction in his life, these words rang true. Most of the hardship he had experienced could be attributed to whites, and he had read much about the horrors of slavery in the Americas and about European colonialism in Africa. But what captivated him most was the idea of a black cultural history, one whose roots were established in ancient Africa, long before the European slave trade. He was not the isolated misfit he had believed himself to be, but part of a proud race with a rich heritage going back thousands of years.

The Nation gave Malcolm the hammer with which to pound out his rage. He began studying Muhammad's teachings with a zeal that would endure for many years, and with his new beliefs came a renewed determination to improve his mind. His regimen of self-improvement was in keeping with the Nation's credo of discipline: mental, spiritual, and moral.

Malcolm worked tirelessly to improve his writing skills, spending hours in the prison library poring over books about religion, history, philosophy, science, archaeology, and spirituality. To the amazement of prison authorities, he became courteous and respectful to inmates and guards. He informed prison officials that he had dropped his "slave name" of Little and had replaced it with the letter X. From then on, he would be known as Malcolm X.

By this time, Elijah Muhammad's program to foster economic independence for African Americans had yielded results. He had opened several businesses in Chicago, and membership in the Nation was steadily increasing. To accommodate its greater numbers, the Nation secured a former animal hospital building for its Chicago headquarters.

Eventually Malcolm X wrote a letter to Elijah Muhammad in which he expressed his deep devotion to his newfound faith. Muhammad answered the letter promptly, welcoming his new charge into the fold and enclosing with his response a five-dollar bill, a customary gesture of goodwill toward prisoners who joined the Nation.

In August 1952, Malcolm X's exemplary behavior earned him an early release from prison, and he headed immediately for his brother Wilfred's home in Detroit. There he became active in the operation of the Nation's Temple Number One, established by Fard and Muhammad nearly 20 years earlier. Soon after, he went to Chicago to meet Muhammad and hear him preach. The new recruit was nearly overwhelmed with awe for the man who was said to be the Messenger of Allah. Muhammad was likewise struck by the enthusiasm of this bright young apostle.

Malcolm X's first meeting with Elijah Muhammad over-whelmed the young disciple. "My worship of him was so awesome," he later said of the Messenger, "that he was the first man whom I had ever feared—not fear such as of a man with a gun, but the fear such as one has of the power of the sun." Malcolm X would become Muhammad's most favored and trusted minister.

One day, Malcolm summoned the nerve to bring to Muhammad's attention the dwindling number of followers attending Temple Number One in Detroit. Muhammad agreed that it was a problem and urged Malcolm X to recruit new members. "Go after the young people," he said. "Once you get them, the older ones will follow through shame."

In recruiting expeditions known to Black Muslims as "fishing," Malcolm X began speaking to people in Detroit's bars and poolrooms and on street corners. Having been an outcast and a criminal himself, Malcolm's keen awareness of their experiences helped him find the precise words to persuade them to reform. Prison inmates, who would hear about the Nation in much the same way as Malcolm had, were particularly attracted to its message and converted in droves. After only a few months, Malcolm managed to triple the membership of Temple Number One, and he would win thousands more converts in the years to come.

The strict moral code and discipline demanded by the Nation of its members deterred many potential converts. But Malcolm X turned these qualities to his advantage. The white man *wants* us to remain disorganized and idle, he would tell his listeners. It is to the white man's advantage that we remain disheartened, because then we are easier to subdue. The words of Malcolm X would stir in African-American ghetto dwellers a sense of outrage and an ardent desire for change.

In 1953, Malcolm X was appointed assistant minister of Temple Number One. By now, he had become a gifted and charismatic speaker. After months of intensive training in Chicago for the ministry, Malcolm X began traveling across the United States, organizing many of the Nation's new temples and visiting those already established. His unquestioning devotion to the teachings of Muhammad, combined with his articulately stated anger at the black man's condition, inspired old members and new converts wherever he went.

During the 1950s, the Nation expanded at a tremendous pace. The organization began to hold national meetings. Declaring February 26—Fard's birthday—"Savior's Day," the Nation drew thousands of members to Chicago for the annual celebration. It also staged huge rallies, called Living Fountain assemblies, in many cities. By the end of the decade, the movement had 50 temples in operation. And although the Nation was reluctant to disclose its membership, estimates in the late 1950s and early 1960s showed at least 50,000 believers, of whom 10 to 30 percent were registered followers; many thousands more who were not affiliated with the movement were sympathizers with the Nation's tenets. Much of this growth was attributed to the zealous labor of Malcolm X.

As the Nation of Islam flourished, it became a more established institution than the transitory fringe group many critics had thought it to be. The small-business efforts of the Black Muslims, which had begun with Muhammad's grocery, bakery, and restaurant, now included grocery stores, apartment buildings, factories, farms, cleaning establishments, restaurants, bakeries, and repair-service shops. At one point during the 1950s, the combined wealth of Black Muslim enterprises was estimated at $10 million. By 1960, the Nation owned a half million dollars' worth of real estate in the Chicago area alone. In 1961 the Nation began publishing its own newspaper, *Muhammad Speaks*, a weekly periodical sold by Black Muslim members who received a fraction of the profits. The paper—founded by Malcolm X, who was later appointed editor—eventually became the largest black publication in the country, with a circulation of a half million.

While traveling the country, Malcolm directed his message almost exclusively to African Americans. Thus, while it developed into a national black organization during the 1950s, the Nation of Islam remained largely unknown to white Americans. For the most part, whites were not even aware of the Nation of Islam's existence until April 1957, when a Black Muslim named Hinton Johnson was severely beaten by policemen and taken to a Harlem jail, prompting a furious and voluble response from the Nation.

Malcolm X was in New York at the time of the arrest. Within minutes of hearing the news, he assembled more than 100 members of the Fruit of Islam and marched with them to the Harlem police

Followers of the Nation of Islam wait to hear Elijah Muhammad speak. During the 1950s, the Nation instituted the annual "Savior's Day" celebration, held in Chicago on February 26—Wallace Fard's birthday. The conventions, still held today, draw thousands of Black Muslims and many non-members sympathetic to the Nation's teachings.

station. Attracted by the commotion, hundreds more African Americans joined the Black Muslims; by the time they reached the precinct station, the marchers numbered more than 800. Concerned that a race riot would erupt, the police entreatied Malcolm X to help break up the angry crowd. "Guarantee that our brother will get medical treatment," Malcolm demanded. "Pledge that the men who beat him will be punished."

After receiving assurances that the police could be trusted to do what he asked, Malcolm returned to the head of the crowd and, without a word, flicked his hands. The crowd immediately dispersed. A policeman stationed nearby watched in amazement: "No man should have that much power," he said.

Indeed, Malcolm X had not only galvanized African Americans outside the small community of the Nation; he had finally succeeded in drawing the attention—and the animosity—of whites as well.

Muhammad Speaks
Powell Says:
FREEDOM
CAN'T WAIT!
Truth Is
The Best
Hits Slow
Pace At
Big Rally
Randolph Warns on

5

"I'm Coming Up!"

HAVING GAINED A larger audience, Malcolm escalated his verbal attacks on "the white devil." The spotlight on the Nation of Islam intensified in 1959 when an African-American journalist, Louis Lomax, acquired Muhammad's consent to make a television documentary on the Black Muslims.

Members of the Nation were pleased that their organization had merited national media coverage. They presumed that such widespread publicity would help to promote the Nation of Islam's teachings and attract new followers.

But they soon learned otherwise. Entitled "The Hate that Hate Produced," the television program, narrated by journalist Mike Wallace, vividly depicted the deep resentment the Black Muslims and their supporters felt for white society, and presented graphic evidence that a storm of rebellion was gathering in the black ghettos of America. Most white Americans were shocked and horrified to learn of the intense bitterness African Americans felt toward them; they were appalled to hear that blacks thought them the embodiment of evil. The scorching words of Malcolm X, which peppered the documentary, filled them with fear, guilt, and distaste.

Malcolm X holds a copy of the Nation of Islam's newspaper, Muhammad Speaks, *during a New York City rally in 1963. The Nation had begun to attract the attention of the media—and of whites in America—with the airing of a 1959 television documentary that presented its black separatist doctrine.*

The Nation of Islam began drawing the country's attention at a time when racial discrimination was one of the most hotly debated issues in America. During the 1950s, while Malcolm X was delivering his fiery message of black separatism to urban ghetto dwellers in the North, a young minister named Martin Luther King, Jr., was leading a boycott of segregated bus services in Montgomery, Alabama. All over the South, civil rights organizations, such as the Southern Christian Leadership Conference (SCLC) and the Congress on Racial Equality (CORE), were challenging racial segregation in public schools and theaters, in restaurants and rest rooms, on trains and buses. Although the nonviolent protest marches led by King and his colleagues often met with brutal retaliation from white policemen and white supremacist organizations, members of the civil rights movement were beginning to feel hope that they could erode racial discrimination in the South.

Like Malcolm X, Martin Luther King, Jr., had grown up in an environment of discrimination. Martin was born in 1929 in Atlanta, Georgia, into a world where blacks attended separate schools and were barred from public facilities such as swimming pools, parks, restaurants, and hotels where whites gathered. African Americans could only attend their own schools and universities, and only with the greatest difficulty could they vote in elections. On sidewalks, they were expected to step aside for whites, and if ever a black were to go inside the home of a white, he or she was to enter by the back door. When African Americans traveled, they passed through bus and train stations with "colored" waiting rooms, water fountains, and toilets on their way to separate railway coaches or seats at the back of the bus.

Like Earl Little, Martin's father was a Baptist minister and an active and courageous campaigner

in the quest for equality, both publicly and in his private life. One day, after having been refused service in a white-owned shoe store because he would not sit in the rear of the shop, Martin's father stormed out onto the sidewalk and angrily declared to his son, "I don't care how long I have to live with this system, I am never going to accept it. I'll oppose it till the day I die!"

Although King's childhood and family were very different from that of Malcolm X, he too suffered the pain and outrage of discrimination. On his return home from a summer job in Hartford, Connecticut, the teenaged Martin was escorted by a

While civil rights activists of the 1950s and 1960s fought the kind of segregation depicted here, the Nation of Islam wanted to form a separate state for blacks within the United States as restitution for years of slavery and injustice.

waiter to a rear table in the dining car of the train he was riding. The waiter then pulled a curtain around Martin so that whites in the car would not have to see a black man eating. "I felt as though a curtain had dropped on my selfhood," he later recalled.

Martin was expected to follow in his father's footsteps and become a minister, but he had doubts about pursuing this path. He inquired into other professions while attending Morehouse College in Atlanta, an all-male, all-black college that his father and grandfather had attended. But after much study of theology and the Bible, Martin became convinced that profound truths lay behind the teachings of Christianity. In 1948, he was ordained a minister and made assistant at Ebenezer Baptist Church in Atlanta, where his father was pastor.

The 19-year-old minister continued his religious training at the Crozer Seminary in Chester, Pennsylvania. Although he studied widely, exploring the writings of scholars from all over the world, both ancient and modern, he most admired American philosophies of justice. He was inspired by the words of Henry David Thoreau, who rejected the view that obedience to civil law was a citizen's highest responsibility and who advocated nonviolent resistance to oppression. In his 1849 essay, "Civil Disobedience," Thoreau had written, "Under a government which imprisons any unjustly, the true place for a just man is also prison."

One Sunday, King attended a lecture in nearby Philadelphia by Dr. Mordecai W. Johnson. Having recently returned from India, Johnson spoke of the struggle of the Indian people for independence from Great Britain. He praised the labors of the movement's leader, Mahatma Gandhi, who believed strongly in the power of love to bring about social change and who had declared that any action or protest against the British should be peaceful. His philosophy had proved successful two years earlier in 1947, when the British had granted India its freedom.

Martin was deeply moved by the story of Gandhi and his crusade. He was fascinated by the Indian leader's ability to combine principles of love and nonviolence with the strength of a mass movement to end oppression, a concept known as *satyagraha*, or the peaceful defiance of government. Loving one's enemies, Gandhi taught—being prepared to suffer rather than inflict harm—would expose injustice and convince oppressors to end it.

Martin's admiration for Gandhi affected him on a personal level as well. Always charming and well liked, he was nevertheless an intensely emotional child, and his violent mood swings persisted through his adulthood. For him, the principles of nonviolence and love for others ran far deeper than his desire for social change. In later years, as King assumed the mantle of leadership for the growing civil rights movement, not even death threats and the bombing of his own home—in which his wife and children narrowly escaped being killed—could deter him from his faith in nonviolence. "We must love our white brothers no matter what they do to us," he told an angry crowd of blacks gathered outside his home after the bombing. "We must make them know that we love them." The crowd dispersed quietly.

Civil rights activists like King won much praise for their courageous fight for racial integration—but not from Malcolm X. He openly scorned their goals and tactics. "You can sit down next to white folks—on the toilet," he remarked, belittling recent rulings outlawing segregated rest rooms. He had nothing but contempt for would-be white allies and had no use for African Americans who believed in an integrated society. He could not abide the idea of imploring whites to provide basic human rights for

Martin Luther King, Jr., with his wife, Coretta, before his trial in March 1956 for violating an Alabama state law forbidding boycotts. King's vision of a peacefully integrated America was inspired by Mahatma Gandhi's concept of nonviolent revolution and by the Christian ideal of love for one's enemies.

those who should already have them. Nor did he believe whites would voluntarily accord blacks these rights.

Instead, Elijah Muhammad and Malcolm X began speaking of a separate state for blacks within the United States, as Wallace Fard had done years earlier. "The Negro must think in terms of bettering himself, and this he can only do by thinking in terms of his own black civilization," Muhammad told a *New York Times* reporter in 1963. When slavery was legally abolished in 1865, the government had promised every freed slave 40 acres of land and a mule as compensation for the injustices each had suffered. A century later, African Americans still had not been vindicated. Muhammad was specific in his demands for restitution: "We believe that our former slave-masters are obligated to maintain and supply our needs in this separate territory for the next 20 to 25 years—until we are able to produce and supply our own needs." And Malcolm X, opposing King's peaceful protest methods and vision of a fully integrated and peaceful society, called on African Americans to fight for their constitutional rights and defend themselves without hesitation when attacked—bullet for bullet, if necessary.

Such violent exhortations and cries for a separate state unsettled and angered not only a great number of whites but also many blacks, especially those who adhered to the philosophy of peaceful revolution. Bayard Rustin, a civil rights leader and organizer, debated with Malcolm X and accused him of indulging in emotionalism. Malcolm shot back, "When a man is hanging on a tree and he cries out, should he cry out unemotionally? This is what you tell black people in this country when they begin to cry out against the injustices that they're suffering . . . . But when a man is on a hot stove, he says, 'I'm coming up. I'm getting up.' Violently or nonviolently doesn't even enter into the picture—'I'm coming up, do you understand?'"

True to his earlier antagonism toward established religion, Malcolm X attacked African-American clergymen with particular vehemence, claiming that they "disarm[ed] the oppressed black masses with a doctrine of cowardice disguised as 'Christian love.'" Determined to draw the attention of the African-American community to what he believed were the dangers of the Christian message, he accused black preachers of subscribing to a "parrot" religion: "[I]s the Negro clergy being paid to disarm our people with the slave master's one-sided religion?" he asked. Black Christian ministers, he said, had become "the willing tools of the very white man who is responsible for our downtrodden people's wretched condition."

Once the general public became aware, through media coverage, of the Nation's white-man-as-devil

Malcolm X addressing Black Muslims in 1963. A fiery and charismatic speaker, this favorite disciple of Elijah Muhammad attracted hundreds of converts even before his 1962 appointment as official spokesperson for the Nation of Islam.

teachings, members of the organization found it increasingly difficult to rent and purchase church halls and other accommodations to hold meetings and establish new temples. In July of 1957, Roy Wilkins, the executive secretary for the NAACP, issued an official statement blasting Muhammad's radical stance: "For years the NAACP has been opposed to white extremists for preaching hatred of Negro people, and we are equally opposed to Negro extremists preaching against white people simply for the sake of whiteness."

Nevertheless, Black Muslims remained adamantly opposed to desegregation and were insulted by the Christian philosophy of turning the other cheek. Such attitudes, the Nation believed, encouraged self-hate, the greatest crime possible against oneself and one's own kind. Moreover, living in an integrated society with the ancestors of slave owners was an abomination to Black Muslims. The white man was doomed—his 6,000 years of dominion were at an end—and any black man who integrated with the corrupt white world would be destroyed along with it. The solution, said Black Muslims, was complete separation of blacks from whites.

Paradoxically, the idea of a separate state for African Americans appealed not only to Black Muslims but also to people who, under different circumstances, might as soon have come after them with a hangman's noose. In June 1961, George Lincoln Rockwell, head of the American Nazi party, a white supremacist group, attended a Black Muslim rally in Washington, D.C., to offer his support against racially mixed marriages. Like the white supremacists of Marcus Garvey's time, the American Nazis' interest in separatism stemmed from a desire not to see African Americans attain equality but to remove them from the country entirely.

Other challenges awaited the Black Muslims. Prison authorities had begun prohibiting incarcerated members of the Nation from practicing their religion. After some of the inmates protested, the Nation filed suits, and two cases were heard by the U.S. Supreme Court. In one case, Black Muslim inmates in California claimed a violation of the Fourteenth Amendment, which guarantees freedom of religion. In the other case, Black Muslims in a New York prison accused authorities of violating the Civil Rights Act of 1871, which maintains that all citizens may practice their chosen religion without government interference. In both cases, the Supreme Court ruled that it was "constitutionally permissable" to deny Black Muslims the right to practice their religion because it threatened national security.

Soon after these decisions, the FBI tightened its surveillance of the Nation, which it had begun in 1941. Government officials were especially concerned with the Fruit of Islam, the Nation's highly trained military corps. Believing that Muhammad was raising his own army, the federal agents wire-tapped members' telephones and placed some of them under surveillance.

By this time, Muhammad's health had begun to deteriorate. Malcolm X had already captured America's attention with the airing of Mike Wallace's 1959 television documentary. Always smartly dressed, stately, and with a gift for blazing rhetoric, Malcolm X was an imposing figure. Journalists and television crews sought him out whenever they needed a statement by the Black Muslims. Although Malcolm X—properly—always advised the media to consult Muhammad directly, Muhammad was a small, reserved, soft-spoken man who lacked the commanding, telegenic presence of his disciple. The media continued to spotlight Malcolm X.

In 1962, Malcolm X became the official spokesperson of the Nation of Islam when Muhammad appointed him national minister of the movement. Although Muhammad retained ultimate control over the Nation, Malcolm X was now formally recognized not only as acting head of the movement but as heir apparent to Elijah. After Malcolm's appointment, Muhammad, on his doctor's advice, moved temporarily with his family from Chicago to Phoenix, Arizona.

Conflicts arose within the Nation's ranks not long after Muhammad's departure. Malcolm X's appointment had aroused the resentment of other officers, notably John Ali, the Nation's head of public relations, and Raymond Sharrieff, Muhammad's son-in-law and the leader of the Fruit of Islam. At

first, Malcolm X only overheard rumors claiming
that he was trying to seize power from Muhammad.
But soon he began to suspect that his rivals were
turning the Messenger himself against him.

6

"A Terrible Cross-Fire"

THOUGH MUHAMMAD'S POSITION as divine Messenger remained unchallenged, his absence from the Nation of Islam's Chicago headquarters created an unintended split in the organization's center of authority. Many Nation of Islam officials, mindful of negative media attention and of FBI surveillance, advocated a more moderate image for the organization than the strong "anti-white" sentiment expressed by Malcolm X, and they urged Muhammad to reemphasize the Nation's economic programs.

In April 1962, antagonism among the Nation's Chicago leaders reached a head when a confrontation between Black Muslims and police in Los Angeles left one member dead and 12 others wounded. Outraged, Malcolm X wanted to retaliate "bullet for bullet" by attacking the police. But in an

One of the worst civil rights disturbances in American history began on August 11, 1965, when the black ghetto of Watts in southeast Los Angeles exploded in violence following a confrontation between a young African American and a white police officer. During six days of rioting, 34 people were killed and thousands were injured; fires like the blaze shown here destroyed scores of homes and businesses.

effort to avoid further conflict with authorities, Muhammad and the other leaders of the Nation forbade him to take action.

Disappointed by the Nation's passive response to blatant police brutality, many young members who had been recruited by Malcolm X left the Nation. And although he strenuously denied any differences between himself and Muhammad, Malcolm X began to express his increasing frustration with what he believed were the Nation's exclusively religious teachings.

Malcolm also remained unimpressed with actions taken by other opponents of prejudice. Civil rights groups achieved a number of victories during the early 1960s: they succeeded in persuading Congress to pass several important bills outlawing discriminatory practices, among them the Civil Rights Act of 1964 and the Economic Opportunity Act. To Malcolm X, though, such reforms could not even come close to achieving concrete improvements in the lives of African Americans. He repeatedly cited as examples of continuing dissatisfaction recent outbreaks of racial violence in response to peaceful protests in Nashville, Birmingham, Atlanta, and Albany. At any moment, Malcolm X insisted, such unrest could explode into widespread rioting.

But civil rights leaders had similar objections to the Nation of Islam: while many people, black and white, were risking their lives for equality under the law, the Nation remained a conservative organization whose only political goal was not to secure equality but to establish a separate black homeland. To civil rights activists, it was the Nation whose angry protests and avoidance of political activism seemed insubstantial and ineffective.

Such criticism was not lost on Malcolm X himself. After the police attack on Black Muslims in 1962, he had begun to believe that the Nation's tenets of separatism and defiance of the white man's

government were not enough to change the condition of African Americans. Neither integration nor separatism alone, he was beginning to believe, would eliminate racial injustice. Increasingly, he began to view the Nation of Islam's teachings as an alternative message of hope rather than a reactionary response to that of the civil rights movement. In his public addresses, he began to emphasize political matters rather than religious issues, and he urged Elijah Muhammad to sanction a more active protest role for the Nation—including, if necessary, the mass protest methods of the civil rights advocates themselves.

Muhammad refused, insisting upon complete isolation from whites in accordance with Black Muslim teaching. Soon after, the Nation stripped Malcolm X of his responsibilities as editor of *Muhammad Speaks*, the movement's newspaper. Elijah's son Herbert ordered staff members to reduce

Malcolm addresses a Harlem rally shortly after announcing his departure from the Nation of Islam on March 8, 1964. In an overture toward the civil rights movement he had previously denounced, he declared that his new organization would "expand the civil rights program to the human rights program" while maintaining a militant philosophy.

the paper's coverage of Malcolm X's activities as well. Under sway of his Chicago officials, Muhammad eventually forbade Malcolm X to appear on television news broadcasts.

As always, Malcolm X deferred to the Messenger's orders and submitted to the restraints put upon him by the Nation, despite his growing desire for political involvement. But by 1963, all his thoughts of reforming the Nation of Islam were pushed aside by turbulence within the organization itself.

In July 1963, two former secretaries of Elijah Muhammad served him with paternity suits, claiming that he was the father of their four children. This news shook Malcolm X's faith in the Nation to its core. Adultery is a grave violation of Black Muslim doctrine—Malcolm's own brother Reginald had been expelled because of it—and it was unthinkable that the divine Messenger of Allah had committed such transgressions. Malcolm X questioned the two women and was stunned not only to hear evidence to support their charges, but also to learn of Muhammad's conviction that Malcolm X had turned against him.

Deeply distressed, Malcolm X traveled to the Messenger's home in Phoenix, determined to hear him out. To Malcolm's dismay, Muhammad did not deny the women's accusations. Instead, he justified his actions as the fulfillment of prophecy by comparing himself to the biblical David and Noah, who had committed similar acts. Unsatisfied with this defense, Malcolm X nonetheless accepted Muhammad's explanation and returned to Chicago to warn other Black Muslim ministers of media reaction to the lawsuit. But many of them perceived his warning as further proof of his treachery—he was spreading vicious stories about the Messenger to advance his own standing, they believed—and the rift between Muhammad and Malcolm X widened.

Nevertheless, despite infighting among Black

Muslim leaders and the bad blood he had generated between himself and the majority of mainstream African-American leaders, Malcolm X remained the primary force behind militant black activism for the urban poor. When, in August 1963, nearly a quarter of a million people took part in a civil rights demonstration called the March on Washington for Jobs and Freedom, Malcolm X—repressing his growing conviction of the power of the civil rights movement—dubbed the event the "Farce on Washington." "I don't believe we're going to overcome [by] singing," he told reporters. "If you're going to get yourself a .45 and start singing 'We Shall Overcome,' I'm with you."

Such inflammatory remarks further widened the gulf between Malcolm X and the Nation until finally the breach was irreparable. On November 22, 1963, President John F. Kennedy was assassinated in Dallas, Texas. While the country mourned the loss of its leader, Muhammad, aware of Kennedy's immense popularity and fearful of violence against Black Muslims should they speak specifically of Kennedy, warned his ministers not to comment on the murder. Indeed, in *Muhammad Speaks*, he praised Kennedy and attributed his death to the his advocacy of African-American equality: "it seems very strange," Muhammad wrote, "that every president who says something favorable for the so-called Negro pays for it with his life."

Malcolm X's first public address after the event came on December 1, 1963, and concerned the imminent destruction and judgment of white America. Although he referred several times to Kennedy, Malcolm X followed Muhammad's orders and did not directly mention the assassination. After the speech, however, when asked by reporters to comment on Kennedy's death, Malcolm X replied that white America was finally being repaid for fostering a "climate of hate." Smiling broadly, he said, "Being

Malcolm X and Martin Luther King, Jr., in 1964. Even before departing from the Nation of Islam, Malcolm X had begun to believe that achieving freedom for American blacks would require compromise rather than separatism.

an old farm boy myself, chickens coming home to roost never did make me sad; they've always made me glad."

Malcolm X's callous comment provoked a national uproar and fed the flames of resentment and bitterness toward the Nation of Islam that had flared up in recent years. Though still ailing, Elijah Muhammad had become wary of Malcolm's power and recognized a convenient moment to deal with this supposed threat to his leadership. He summoned his disciple to Phoenix. "That was a very bad statement," he told Malcolm X. "The country loved this man. . . . A statement like that can make it hard on Muslims in general." He suspended Malcolm X from his duties as national minister for 90 days, during which time he was not to speak to the press.

Once again, the young minister dutifully accepted his punishment in the hope of mending his tattered relationship with the Nation. In the throes of a spiritual crisis, he traveled with his family to Florida for a holiday during his suspension. While there, Malcolm X visited with a popular young professional boxer named Cassius Clay, who had not yet announced publicly that he had converted to the Nation of Islam and changed his name to Muhammad Ali. Hoping that his association with the boxer would help repair the rift between himself and Elijah Muhammad by winning positive publicity for the Nation of Islam, Malcolm X helped prepare Clay for his heavyweight title bout against the reigning champion, Sonny Liston. Despite Malcolm X's hopes, however, Ali's victory over Liston and the announcement of his conversion did little to improve Malcolm X's standing with the Nation.

In January 1964, Malcolm X was summoned to Chicago to face charges by Nation of Islam officials that he was planning a rebellion against Elijah Muhammad; he was relieved of his duties as minister of Temple Number Seven. At the same time, Muhammad excommunicated his son Wallace for what he believed was Wallace's complicity with Malcolm X's plan.

While in Chicago, Malcolm X was further shocked to learn from a member of Temple Number Seven that a high-ranking Black Muslim official had ordered the man to assassinate him. He had often received death threats from members of white hate groups, but the idea that his Black Muslim brothers would conspire to kill him was devastating. "I could conceive death. I couldn't conceive betrayal—not of the loyalty which I had given to the Nation of Islam, and to Mr. Muhammad," he would relate in his autobiography. "I felt like something in *nature* had failed—like the sun or the stars."

Malcolm X decided he had no choice but to follow his conscience. On March 8, 1964, he formally announced his departure from the Nation of Islam, declaring that he was establishing his own movement, called Muslim Mosque Incorporated. His original intent was to remain faithful to the teachings of Muhammad, but he also made it clear from the start that Muslim Mosque was to be a revolutionary group, "the working base for an action program designed to eliminate the political oppression, the economic exploitation, and the social degradation suffered daily by 22 million Afro-Americans." The Muslim Mosque's charter members, numbering about 50 people, were former supporters of the Nation, but Malcolm X welcomed blacks of all religious denominations. And—having begun to reflect on the successes of the integrationist civil rights movement—for the first time he invited whites to contribute money and ideas to his organization as well (though whites were not permitted to join the Muslim Mosque).

Malcolm stressed that, despite his break with Elijah Muhammad, he would not abandon his phi-

Philbert X (left), brother of Malcolm X, with James Shabazz, denounces his brother as a hypocrite and traitor for breaking with the Nation of Islam in 1964. When Malcolm was imprisoned from 1946 to 1952, Philbert had joined Reginald Little and sister, Hilda, in persuading Malcolm to reform by becoming a follower of Muhammad.

losophy of militancy. And though he had begun to acknowledge the advances made by the civil rights movement and its manner of mass protest, he refused to adopt their passive resistance methods. He maintained that it was "criminal" to advocate nonviolence in the face of routine violence perpetrated against African Americans. Malcolm X's aim instead was to expand the civil rights movement, to broaden its boundaries to include self-defense, and to eliminate racial injustice and oppression of blacks "by any means necessary."

Less than a month after he formed the Muslim Mosque, Malcolm X went on a spiritual pilgrimage, or *hajj*, to Mecca. His experiences there completely transformed him. Traditional Islam, he learned, had no place for the concept of black separatism and disapproved of racial hatred. He spoke and prayed with European Muslims "whose eyes were the bluest of blue, whose hair was the blondest of blond, and whose skin was the whitest of white." As a result, his harsh view of whites softened considerably. He was "spellbound," he said, by the "overwhelming spirit of true brotherhood" that he saw among "people *of all colors.*" He concluded that the white man is "*not inherently evil,*" but that "America's racist society influences him to act evilly." In an open letter to the American press, he wrote that the "overwhelming spirit of true brotherhood" that he saw while on his pilgrimage forever changed his views on race and religion.

Malcolm X's trip also took him to Egypt, Arabia, Lebanon, Algeria, Nigeria, and Ghana, where he reconfirmed his conviction that the African-American freedom movement was inseparable from the struggles of blacks in Africa—indeed, the struggles of blacks around the world. Upon his return to the United States in June 1964, Malcolm X changed his name to El Hajj Malik El-Shabazz to reflect his conversion to Orthodox Islam.

While Malcolm X made his *hajj,* the repercussions of his departure rippled through the Nation of Islam, triggering further discord between members who had sympathized with Malcolm X and those who denounced him. Akbar, one of Elijah Muhammad's sons, attacked his father's teaching as "politically sterile" and charged the Nation with moral and religious bankruptcy; Muhammad excommunicated him shortly after expelling his son Wallace. A few months later, Hassan Sharrieff, a grandson of Muhammad, announced his resignation from the movement, describing his grandfather as a "fake and a fraud."

Once it became clear that there would be no reconciliation between Malcolm X—now Malik Shabazz—and the Nation of Islam, its leaders launched a savage attack on him. His brothers Wilfred X and Philbert X ran a series of articles in *Muhammad Speaks,* calling Malcolm X a hypocrite and a traitor. Lawyers of the Nation sued in an attempt to reclaim the title to his house in East Elmhurst, New York, where he lived with his wife, Betty, and his daughters.

Malcolm X did not hesitate to respond to such assaults, calling Muhammad a fraud and referring to his time as a Black Muslim as "a mistake." Moreover, the Nation, Malcolm X charged, was ignoring the opportunity to advance the black cause and work with other civil rights organizations. During the "Freedom Summer" of 1964, America was aflame with racial violence. Black southern churches were firebombed, and civil rights marchers were jailed and battered by police. In Mississippi, three activists—one black man and two white men—were beaten and shot to death. Riots erupted in New York, Chicago, Philadelphia, and other northern cities. How could the Nation of Islam stand by and refuse to take action against these horrors?

Such challenges only intensified the Nation's anger toward Malcolm X. Near the end of 1964, a number of his aides were attacked and beaten by members of the Nation. Another group of followers were assaulted by Black Muslims while in their car in a Boston tunnel. Malcolm X himself was under surveillance by the FBI and by the Nation, and he began to suspect that the two organizations were in collusion against him. In December, he received a series of death threats, and two months later he was deported from France, where he had planned to speak at a Paris rally, on the grounds that he was a security threat. He had begun to feel like a hunted man.

During this time, Elijah Muhammad continued to emphasize the Nation's doctrine of the "Fall of America." According to Wallace Fard's legend of Yakub, the 6,000-year rule over the world by the "white devils" was coming to an end. Its demise had begun at the onset of World War I, the "War of the Anti-Christs." Now, 50 years later, there would be no turning back. For Muhammad, the social and economic upheavals and the threat of atomic war in America were clear signs that this country would be the first to fall. Malcolm's traitorous behavior and the Nation's internal conflicts were more immediate—and prophetic—signs. Minister Louis X (later Louis Farrakhan) declared that Malcolm had "fulfill[ed] the prophetic role of Korah, the . . . one who rebelled against the leadership of Moses because he coveted Moses' position."

Malcolm X's home was firebombed in mid-February 1965. A week after the bombing, on February 21, he was scheduled to speak at a meeting of the Organization for Afro-American Unity (OAAU), a nonreligious offshoot of his new movement. Introduced as a "man who would give his life for you," Malcolm X had no sooner greeted his audience than he was gunned down by three men who rushed the stage.

One of the assailants, Talmadge Hayer, was apprehended immediately. He denied any connection with the Nation or with the other assassins, although all three were later convicted of the murder and identified as Black Muslims. Elijah Muhammad and the Nation disavowed involvement. Many believed otherwise or speculated that the Central Intelligence Agency (CIA), the FBI, or white supremacist organizations were involved or had conspired with the Nation. Though theories persist, the identity of the people who arranged the assassination of Malcolm X remains a mystery.

On February 22, the day after the shooting, the Nation of Islam mosque in Harlem was bombed. The following afternoon, a Black Muslim building in San Francisco was set on fire. That same day— just two days after the shooting—the New York City headquarters of Muslim Mosque Incorporated was firebombed. Not long after, the organization founded by El Hajj Malik El-Shabazz—Malcolm X—in the hope of bridging the gap between militant separatism and political activism dissolved.

Not surprisingly, the death of the estranged

Malcolm X's widow, Betty, and mourners listen while Islamic prayers are recited for the slain leader. In the year before his death on February 21, 1965, Malcolm X made a pilgrimage to Mecca and changed his name to El Hajj Malik El-Shabazz to reflect his conversion to traditional Islam.

national minister received little official attention from the Nation of Islam. Although *Muhammad Speaks* ran a few brief articles on Malcolm X, they were filled with regret not for his violent death but for the "role he had unfortunately chosen to play since his separation from the Nation of Islam." In other articles, Malcolm X's defection from the Nation of Islam was cited as further proof of the imminent Fall of America, the end of the white man's rule: "All signs of the times point to the fact that the day of judgment . . . has already dawned and that the black man in America is caught in its terrible cross-fire," read the cover article of one edition.

During his address at the annual Savior's Day celebration in Chicago five days after the killing, Elijah Muhammad described Malcolm X as a "star who had gone astray." Wallace Muhammad, one of Elijah's sons, had been excommunicated for being in league with Malcolm in January 1964, shortly before Malcolm X broke from the movement. Now, before a national assembly of Black Muslims, he repented for having joined against his father. "I want to make a confession of guilt for having made a public dispute which I should have taken up privately," he said during the assembly. "I judged my father when I should have let God do it. I regret my mistake."

Malcolm X had played a critical role in transforming the Nation of Islam from an exotic fringe group to a national organization. His firm belief in Black Muslim doctrine and his gift of persuasion had won thousands of converts to the Nation. And when his experiences with the American civil rights movement and his pilgrimage to Mecca began to convince him of a brotherhood much broader and more accepting than that of the Nation he had abandoned, many of his followers would echo his call for sweeping changes in the black nationalist movement and would leave the Nation as Malcolm X himself had been compelled to do.

But other Black Muslim officials who had been devoted to Malcolm X's brand of activism—and who had since come to regard him as a "traitor"— were gathered around the Messenger that Savior's Day in 1965. Among them was a young minister whom Malcolm X had called "little brother," who had, like Malcolm X, risen quickly through the ranks of the organization and was destined to revolutionize the Nation of Islam—Louis Farrakhan.

7

The Charmer

Louis Farrakhan during a press conference at the Nation of Islam mosque in Harlem. A favorite disciple of Malcolm X, Farrakhan quickly ascended through the Nation's ranks, becoming a minister only two years after converting in 1955.

LOUIS FARRAKHAN—LOUIS X—had been in the Nation's Newark temple on the day that Malcolm X died, filling in there while its minister, James Shabazz, replaced Malcolm X in the New York temple. Though Louis X had been a cherished colleague of Malcolm, he had lost more than half of the members of his Boston temple after Malcolm's defection from the Nation of Islam and was his most outspoken adversary in the months following the rift. Now, at the Savior's Day assembly days after Malcolm X's assassination, Louis X, who had become one of Elijah Muhammad's most trusted advisors, was poised to assume the ministry of the New York temple—and later the leadership of the Nation of Islam.

Boston was already home to eight-year-old Louis Eugene Walcott when the angry teenager named Malcolm Little had first arrived in 1941. Like Malcolm, Gene was raised without a father. Both boys suffered the alienation of being lighter skinned than other family members. Gene's mother, Sara Mae, a Caribbean immigrant, struggled to provide for her family on her own during the Depression years, just as Louise Little had done for her family. Both had managed to subsist through welfare payments and odd jobs whenever they were available.

But the similarities ended there. The Roxbury section of Boston, where the Walcotts lived, was a close-knit community of West Indian immigrants that offered at least some measure of unity and security against ever-present ethnic and racial tensions. Mae raised her two sons with a strict hand, always stressing the importance of education, music, and religion. Gene would not suffer the devastations upon his family and the frustration and anger that would draw the young Malcolm into delinquency and crime. He felt at home and safe in Roxbury and was a bright, diligent student.

Gene was an active member of St. Cyprian's Episcopal Church, which had been established by the black Caribbeans of Boston. In addition to serving as an acolyte (a minister's assistant) and singing in the choir, he regularly played his violin at Sunday concerts. But the young churchgoer could not understand "why it was an honor to go downtown to sing with a white choir in a white church." He would wonder "why, if God had sent a deliverer to an oppressed people in the past, why that same God wouldn't send *us* a deliverer? I never heard my pastor speak on the question of the liberation of my people. . . . I loved Jesus and I loved scripture, but I just wanted answers."

Although Sara Mae Walcott was not a member of Marcus Garvey's UNIA, the organization maintained a strong presence among Caribbean immigrants, and Gene was introduced to it at an early age. While visiting his uncle in New York, the 11-year-old noticed a picture of a black man on the mantlepiece and asked who he was. "The greatest leader our people ever had," replied his uncle, explaining the teachings of Garvey. When Gene asked where this man could be found, his uncle told him he had died. Farrakhan later described his sorrow over the news:

A symbolic coffin burns during a June 1967 protest against racial violence in the Roxbury section of Boston. The rally took place in the neighborhood where Louis Farrakhan—and Malcolm X—grew up and where Farrakhan later assumed leadership of the city's Nation of Islam mosque.

"[I] was so hurt that after hoping, all my young years, to meet the right man for our people, that when I found him, he was already dead . . . I cried and cried because Marcus Garvey was dead."

When Gene was 16, a New York calypso group, the Calypsonians, came to Roxbury for a fundraising concert. A musician himself, Gene was struck by the new sound. "I can do that," he said to a friend, and soon he was. That same year, he began performing in the city's black nightclubs as "The Charmer."

Gene continued his studies while he performed, and in 1950 he entered Winston-Salem Teachers' College in North Carolina. Traveling south, he encountered for the first time the horrors of official segregation and overt racism. During a stopover between trains, he was turned away from a movie theater; "We don't sell tickets to niggers," one theater employee told him. When he arrived in North Carolina, he discovered separate water fountains and bathroom facilities for whites and blacks, something he had never seen in the North despite the racial and ethnic tension of immigrant Boston.

Walcott remained devoted to music, practicing his violin for hours each day and organizing a calypso band that gave statewide concerts. During his second year of college, he heard about a young African-American calypso singer named Harry Belafonte whose music was quickly becoming popular across the country. Frustrated with his own progress as a performer, he decided to drop out of college and pursue a music career. In 1953 he married Betty Ross, whom he had met the previous year, and they settled in Boston.

Two years later, when Gene and Betty Walcott were in Chicago for an eight-week musical tour, they ran into an old friend, a recent convert to the Nation of Islam. He persuaded the couple to attend the Nation's annual gathering in that city.

Sitting in the balcony listening to Elijah Muhammad, Farrakhan recalls, he was impressed by Muhammad's ideas but did not think much of the man's uneducated way of speaking. All at once, Muhammad looked up toward Walcott and said, "Brother, don't pay attention to how I speak. Pay attention to what I'm saying. I didn't get the chance to go to the white man's fine schools, because when I tried to go, the doors were closed. But if you take what I say and place it into the beautiful way of speaking you know, you can help me save our people." Walcott, understandably, was shocked.

Later, however, he would learn that Muhammad was informed of the "college man" in the audience "who could help us if we get him," and knew where he would be sitting. At that moment, however, Walcott was astounded, convinced that the Messenger could read his mind. Nevertheless, when he joined the movement that day, he was still unsure of his decision. Not until several months later, when, as a new convert to the Nation he first heard Malcolm X speak, was he certain that he had chosen the right path.

For Walcott, now named Louis X, the Nation provided both a mission—to inspire and uplift his fellow African Americans—and a platform from which to do it. In May 1957, only a few months after his return to Boston as a captain of the Fruit of Islam, Louis X was appointed minister of the city's temple.

True to Elijah Muhammad's belief in reaching out to the downtrodden and the outcast, the members of Temple Number Eleven in Boston included former convicts, drug addicts, prostitutes, and juvenile delinquents. But perhaps because Boston is home to several colleges and universities, the temple also attracted more than the usual number of college-educated converts. A former entertainer—and college dropout—Louis X struggled to overcome his discomfort with these college graduates, whom he believed were "much more intelligent" than he was.

Malcolm X, a self-educated man, now minister of Temple Number Seven in New York, would frequently travel to Boston to speak at Louis X's temple. He would often reassure the young minister that teaching the truth of the Nation of Islam did not require an advanced academic degree. With Malcolm X's encouragement, Louis X tripled the temple's membership within five years.

Residents of Roxbury who had known Louis X as The Charmer were surprised by the solemn atmosphere of the Nation's gatherings. But the entertainer in Louis X had not disappeared: not long after his appointment to the ministry, he cut a record entitled "White Man's Heaven is a Black Man's Hell." The 10-minute song, an odd combination of intense, accusatory lyrics set to an upbeat calypso rhythm, is a musical "sermon" based on the teachings of Elijah Muhammad. Dancing and music were forbidden to members of the Nation, but perhaps because it was an effective recruiting tool, Muhammad permitted Louis X to spread his message through song. Louis X's song indeed became an unofficial anthem of the organization and was played in the Nation's restaurants and shops across the country, drawing hundreds of new members.

But after Louis had cut another record, "Look at My Chains," and had written two musical plays, *The Trial* and *Orgena* ("a negro" spelled backwards), the Messenger confronted his disciple. "Brother, do you want to be a song-and-dance man or do you want to be my minister?" Louis X quickly adopted the more somber, earnest demeanor of his mentor, Malcolm—the behavior his leader expected of him.

Louis X joined the Nation during the 1950s, a period of prosperity and growth both for the United States and for the Nation, and the organization was establishing itself as a channel for economic success for African Americans. By the early 1960s, when Malcolm X had attained prominence as national minister of the Nation of Islam, seeds of internal discord had grown over rumors about the moral failings of Elijah Muhammad. When a shocked Malcolm X learned of the truth of the rumors from Elijah himself, he sought the opinion of his former "student" and friend, Louis X. He was further dismayed to learn that Louis's faith in the Messenger remained steady.

After Malcolm X left the Nation of Islam, his vehement attacks about the "distorted" and "racist philosophy" of the Nation led to equally scathing countercharges by the Nation's officials. Louis X, the man whom Malcolm X had called "little brother," joined Malcolm's own brothers, Reginald and Philbert, in furiously attacking him. Malcolm X, said Louis X in *Muhammad Speaks,* had "played the hypocrite on both sides" by pretending to be a follower of Muhammad while pandering to the white man. "Only those who wish to be led to hell, or to their doom," he proclaimed, "will follow Malcolm. The die is set, and Malcolm shall not escape. . . . Such a man as Malcolm is worthy of death."

When Malcolm X was assassinated less than three months later, many would remember Louis X's words and link him with the murder. Although Malcolm X had received numerous death threats and

The Nation of Islam Savior's Day rally of 1964, shortly before Malcolm X's official break with the Nation. Elijah Muhammad is applauded by followers, while his wife Clara (left, in white) and Louis X (right, behind podium) look on.

had been branded a traitor by many other followers of the Nation of Islam, none had been so public or vigorous in denouncing him as Louis X.

After hearing of the murder, Farrakhan would say many years later, he walked the streets "reflecting on this man who was my teacher, my mentor. Though I disagreed vehemently with Malcolm's characterization of the honorable Elijah Muhammad, I was not happy that such a man was murdered." Although he disavows direct involvement in the assassination, he has recently acknowledged that his strong denouncements of Malcolm X "helped to create an atmosphere" of condemnation and anger that led to the killing.

Infighting among Black Muslim leaders and adverse publicity had drastically reduced the movement's numbers in the years immediately following Malcolm X's departure. Reports of violence against those who opposed the Nation and rumors of financial mismanagement by Black Muslim officials, which had begun before Malcolm X left, persisted. (Although the Nation's own estimate of membership during the latter half of the 1960s shows a 300-percent increase over the earlier half of the decade, the numbers may reflect an effort to project solidarity and strength in the aftermath of these earlier troubles.)

But larger elements were at work as well. America's disaffected blacks were growing increasingly desperate for change, their frustration exploding in riots across the country. Instead of trying to unify different strands of black separatists, however, Elijah Muhammad chose to keep the Nation out of the public spotlight to avoid further controversy. By the end of the decade, the movement's powerful dominion over the black imagination had begun to wane.

Shortly after the death of Malcolm X, Louis X was appointed minister of the prestigious Temple Number Seven in New York, where Malcolm had preached for years. Though very little violence was reported during Louis X's ministry there, the Nation's detractors—including the FBI—persisted in charging him and other New York officials of the Nation with financial corruption. In August 1968, New York FBI agents published and distributed to Temple Number Seven members an extensive booklet purporting to explain in detail the "high living" and corruption of the temple's ministers. The fact that Louis X dressed in fine clothing, owned expensive cars, and employed a maid for his large home in a predominantly white New York suburb did not help dispel these rumors. Though Louis X was never accused or convicted of wrongdoing by the Nation itself, Elijah Muhammad sent the supreme captain of the Fruit of Islam to the city to investigate the FBI's charges and subsequently issued an order to New York officials for more stringent bookkeeping.

As the 1970s began, the Nation still claimed its share of followers. But—as had happened when Fard disappeared decades earlier—the loss of a strong center of power was beginning to weaken the Nation. Muhammad, in poor health and now permanently residing in Phoenix, was losing his firm grip on the organization. Schemes and rumors had begun circulating among Black Muslim officials over the Messenger's successor. Splinter groups, which disputed Muhammad's theology and questioned the truth of his teachings, had begun to draw followers away from the Nation, and some who left on their own feared that the Nation would exact physical punishment for "desertion."

In October 1971, conflicts over the Nation's leadership and factional disputes over the truth of Muhammad's brand of Islam became violent. Raymond Sharrieff, Elijah Muhammad's son-in-law and chief bodyguard, was shot and wounded outside the office of *Muhammad Speaks*. Three months later, as apparent retribution for the attack, two members of

Fractured by internal conflict among its leaders, the Nation of Islam was rocked with violence in the early 1970s. After this Oklahoma City mosque was shotgunned, presumably by members of a Black Muslim faction, Minister Theodore GX vowed to avenge the destruction by hunting down and killing the perpetrators.

a dissident group, Donald 7X Veira and Freddie 5X Webb, were murdered in their homes. In December of that year, a guard at the Nation's Salaam Restaurant was killed. The violence continued into 1972, when a street battle in Baton Rouge, Louisiana, left four people dead.

Seven of the black men arrested in the Baton Rouge attack were from Chicago, leading to reports that they were members or affiliates of the Nation. Muhammad met with the press shortly after the incident to quell rumors about internal unrest and to deny involvement in the attack, but his words had little impact.

One year later, seven members of a dissident group called the Hanafi Muslims were murdered in their homes in an affluent African-American section of Washington, D.C. Among those killed in the attack were three infants and the 10- and 25-year-old sons of the Hanafi leader, Hamaas Abdul Khaalis; his wife and daughter were shot in the head but survived. Seven Philadelphia Nation of Islam members were convicted of the crimes. Police believed that the murders were committed in revenge because Khaalis had labeled Elijah Muhammad a false prophet. In May 1973, Hakim Jamal, the head of a group called the Malcolm X Foundation, was murdered in his Roxbury home; this too was thought to be retribution for Jamal's condemnation of Elijah Muhammad.

In September, James Shabazz, the minister of the Nation's Temple Number Twenty-Five in Newark, New Jersey, was gunned down by two black men while getting out of his car. Three members of Shabazz's temple kidnapped a black police officer the next day in an attempt to gain information on the murder investigation. (The officer was released after two days.) Two weeks later, the decapitated bodies of two young members of the Newark temple were found in a nearby park.

A short time later, the Newark police arrested 11 members of a group called the New World Order of Islam, who belonged to the Nation's Newark temple. The faction had been feuding with Shabazz, accusing him of overconservativism. Finally, after the arrests, the killings ceased.

It is not certain whether Elijah Muhammad had a clear idea of the brutality growing within the ranks of the Nation. Throughout this period of turmoil, however, he exhorted his followers to refrain from violence and crime: "Just take that which God has given to you and make something out of it. . . . You go to war with no man! No! You go to war with yourself."

But Louis X, whom Muhammad had renamed Louis Farrakhan, delivered a different message.

Commenting upon the death of Minister James Shabazz, he thundered, "It is written in the holy Quran that whosoever kills a Muslim, he must be killed. . . . We are not an evil people. We are lovers of life and we respect the sacredness of life. But he who did not respect the sacredness of the life of [James Shabazz] . . . what right do we have to respect a life like that?"

Ironically, the Nation of Islam was at the same time improving its reputation in the international Islamic community. In May 1972, the Libyan government granted a $3-million loan to the Nation for a new temple in Chicago. Later in the year, government officials from two other Middle East countries, Abu Dabhi and Qatar, presented the Nation with funds to further the cause of Islam in America. An article in *Muhammad Speaks* in October 1972 declared that "[w]idespread financial support of the Lost Found Nation of Islam is now a reality throughout the Islamic world."

In January 1973, the Nation of Islam purchased the Guaranty Bank and Trust Company of South Chicago. Finally, according to *Muhammad Speaks*, the Nation would "show [its] maturity and wisdom" by establishing a black-owned financial institution to complement its business enterprises.

But despite—or perhaps because of—continued expansion, the Nation fell into grave financial difficulty. In part because of Elijah Muhammad's desire to help needy African Americans, many of the older, more established leaders of the Nation were former prisoners or street hustlers, largely uneducated and thus unprepared to manage the growing assets of the Nation. Nevertheless, they held a tight rein on the Nation's economic activities, shutting out younger members and instilling resentment among newcomers.

Although only a small number of the Nation's members engaged in violence, such incidents gar-

The Fruit of Islam surrounds the limousine of Wallace Muhammad during the funeral of his father, Elijah, who died on February 25, 1975.

nered national media attention. Less publicized was the extraordinary shift in Elijah Muhammad's philosophy regarding the future of the Nation of Islam.

During the previous decade, Muhammad had consistently predicted that the demise of the hated white man would occur during the Fall of America. Now, although he continued to speak of an apocalypse, the Messenger seemed to temper his abhorrence of whites and to move closer to the teachings of Orthodox Islam. In his last major speech, on Savior's Day in 1974, Muhammad called upon his followers to have respect for their fellow Muslims *and* for whites. No longer was the black man to blame whites for his condition: "I say that the Black man in North America has nobody to blame but himself. If he respects himself and will do for himself, his once slavemaster will come and respect him and help him to do something for self." Since blacks were responsible for creating whites—according to the myth of Yacub, an evil black scientist invented white people—then they should respect whites.

Muhammad's health worsened, and in January 1975 he was hospitalized. Perhaps because of his efforts at reconciliation with whites, many civic leaders who had condemned Muhammad—or who had been condemned *by* him—publicly praised and commended the man whom polls had called "the most powerful black man in America."

On February 25, 1975—the day before Savior's Day—Elijah Muhammad died of heart failure. The next evening, the Nation of Islam announced the appointment of Wallace Muhammad, Elijah's son, as Supreme Minister of the Nation of Islam (since Elijah had been the divine Messenger of Allah, no other individual could assume his title).

Many were surprised at this choice. After his expulsion from the Nation in 1964, Wallace Muhammad had established the short-lived Afro-Descendent Society of Upliftment, a predominantly political organization aimed at social and economic progress for African Americans. Although he returned to the Nation in 1965 after Malcolm X's death, Wallace had been suspended from the movement twice more before finally being readmitted in 1974.

But Wallace believed that his appointment had been preordained, not by Elijah Muhammad but by divine destiny. During the Savior's Day assembly following his father's death, Wallace assured members of the Nation that he would uphold the teachings of the Messenger. But he also spoke of reconciliation between blacks and whites, as Elijah Muhammad had only begun to do during his final years. "We are not a people who harp upon color or race," he said, in an abrupt departure from the Messenger's original teachings.

Before a huge photograph of his father, Wallace Muhammad rides on the shoulders of his followers after being named the new leader of the Nation of Islam in 1975.

Among those confounded by Wallace's appointment was Louis Farrakhan, whose dedication to the Messenger and swift rise to power among the Nation's officials had led many—including Farrakhan himself—to believe that he had been singled out for leadership by Elijah Muhammad. In an effort to present a united front, Farrakhan, who was at that time minister of New York's Temple Number Seven, swore allegiance to Wallace during the Savior's Day address. But while Farrakhan remained faithful to the original teachings of Allah and the Messenger, it soon became evident that Wallace was determined to make drastic reforms within the Nation of Islam.

8

Turning the Corner

After severing ties with Wallace Muhammad in early 1978, Farrakhan revived the original Nation of Islam and restored many of its practices, including the annual Savior's Day celebration, shown here in 1994. A photograph of Fard is behind Farrakhan.

UPON THE ARREST of Newark's faction members in 1973, the violence and divisiveness within the Nation of Islam ceased, and with the appointment of Wallace Muhammad in 1975, the organization seemed stable and prepared to face new challenges. And the greatest and most demanding challenge came not from outside the Nation but from the Supreme Minister himself.

Shortly after assuming leadership, Wallace began speaking of what he called the Second Resurrection. Traditional Black Muslim doctrine decreed an end to the rule of the "white devil" only after black self-knowledge (the First Resurrection) had been achieved. When the Nation's mission had been to lift up African Americans, Wallace said, it had been necessary to remain separate from the outside world. Now that a black consciousness had been realized, this isolation was no longer efficient or desirable. Wallace dropped the Nation of Islam's traditional demand for a separate black state within America.

Furthermore, he decreed that whites were not intrinsically evil—just as Malcolm X had come to believe in the last years of his life. Rather, it was evil

Wallace Muhammad in his headquarters in Chicago's Temple Number Two. In October 1976, after instituting extensive doctrinal and organizational reforms, Wallace renamed the Nation of Islam the World Community of al-Islam in the West (WCIW).

that "ruled them for their glory and ruled [blacks] for their shame." One hundred days after Elijah Muhammad's death, his son declared whites not devils but "fully human" and invited them to join the Nation of Islam.

With such sweeping doctrinal changes came equally significant organizational reforms. Black Muslims were no longer required to wear the "uniform" of the Nation of Islam—jackets, bow-ties, and clean-shaven faces for men, and neck-to-ankle dresses and veils for women. Savior's Day became "Ethnic Survival Week," commemorating the achievements of African Americans. The Muslims' official publication, *Muhammad Speaks*, renamed by Wallace the *Bilalian News*, ran articles on secular topics such as popular music and ceased publishing the Nation's list of political directives in every issue. To refer to the African-American community, he substituted the word "Bilalian" for "black" in honor of the slave Bilal, appointed by the Islamic founder Muhammad to call the faithful to prayer.

In the summer of 1975, the Nation of Islam hosted a lavish reception in honor of champion boxer Muhammad Ali and attended by a number of celebrities, including musician Stevie Wonder and activist and minister Jesse Jackson. The event marked the first time that smoking and drinking were permitted at a Nation of Islam function.

In 1976, the Supreme Minister publicly disclosed the net worth of the Nation, which had always been a closely kept secret. In an effort to repair the Nation's grave financial situation, he removed his ministers from involvement in business operations and began selling off the Nation's properties. He revised the organization's pay system, setting a $150- to $300-per-week range for each minister, to eliminate competition and corruption among officials.

Perhaps most significantly, to rid the Nation of what he called "spiritual spookiness," Wallace announced that his father no longer would be considered the Messenger of Allah but merely a wise man who had brought the teachings of the Quran to American blacks. Nor was Wallace Fard the incarnation of the Almighty; he was simply the founder of the movement.

Finally, on October 18, 1976, the Nation of Islam itself ceased to exist. In its place would be the World Community of al-Islam in the West (WCIW), a nonracist, nonpolitical group embracing Orthodox Islam. The new organization, said the Supreme Minister, was "a world community" that would include all people. When, in early 1977, Wallace abolished the Fruit of Islam, the Black Muslims' private police force, the last vestige of the organization's political identity vanished.

In less than two years, Wallace Muhammad had radically altered the organization founded by Wallace Fard and built up by Elijah Muhammad, changing the very nature of its mission. Thus, it was no surprise that some longtime members felt resentful and alienated from a movement that had helped shape their lives.

Although outward signs of dissatisfaction were not immediately evident, rumors of a rift in the movement had lingered since the days of Elijah Muhammad. Like Malcolm X, Louis Farrakhan was a powerful minister of the Nation, whose commanding presence often diverted attention from Wallace Muhammad. In June 1975, Wallace removed Farrakhan from his prominent post as minister of Temple Number Seven in New York. He transferred Farrakhan to Chicago, ostensibly to function as "special ambassador" to the Supreme Minister, and assigned him to a small temple in the city's ghetto, effectively limiting Farrakhan's opportunity to preach. Although the move was officially a promotion, some members thought that, as with Elijah Muhammad and Malcolm X, Wallace had grown mistrustful of his celebrated minister and concerned over his increasing influence.

Abdul Haleem Farrakhan, as Wallace renamed him, dutifully complied with the new leader's reforms and urged other members to do the same. "Don't be afraid to reach out for new knowledge. Don't be like the worm that's afraid of the light and wants to keep his head in the darkness," Farrakhan advised his disciples. He remained publicly committed to the new organization even while other veteran members—and many sympathetic outsiders— were skeptical of Wallace's changes.

Privately, though, Farrakhan began to feel the strain of complying with revolutionary new teachings while remaining faithful to the Messenger's philosophy. Particularly trying was the movement's official shift in attitude toward Malcolm X, Farrakhan's mentor. Formerly a reviled traitor to the Nation, Malcolm was now revered by the WCIW as a martyr and a prophet: Harlem's Temple Number Seven, which had flourished under Malcolm X's ministry, was renamed Malcolm Shabazz Temple Seven. Feeling increasingly marginalized and embittered, Farrakhan began to understand the disillusionment Malcolm X had experienced 10 years earlier. "I turned away from Malcolm," he told an interviewer. "Only later did I learn . . . [t]hat I had to walk in his shoes to understand where he was coming from. . . . To be suspect because of a growing popularity, as was Malcolm. To be undermined and vilified as was Malcolm. The only thing I don't want to repeat is the end of Malcolm."

By December 1977, newspapers were reporting a split between the two ministers; even rumors of death threats against Farrakhan surfaced, but they were quickly checked by Wallace. The following January, however, Farrakhan told a *Chicago Tribune* reporter, "I am not welcomed in the World Community of al-Islam in the West and I know it." On March 7, Farrakhan announced to the *New York Times* that he was severing all ties with Wallace Muhammad and the WCIW. Several days later, he declared that he was reviving the original Nation of Islam.

As head of the "new Nation," Farrakhan reinstituted as doctrinal truths the principles of the original movement, based upon the myth of Yacub, the Fall of America, and the vision of Ezekiel's wheel. He resuscitated the Nation's newspaper, *Muhammad Speaks*, renaming it *The Final Call* after Elijah Muhammad's 1934 paper. He rebuilt the Fruit of Islam as an honorable and powerful "army of saviors." To maintain continuity with the old Nation, Farrakhan acquired much of its former property during a protracted legal battle for Elijah Muhammad's

A homeless African American warms himself over a Detroit restaurant vent on a subzero day. The WCIW has increasingly involved itself in efforts to improve the housing and social conditions of urban blacks. By drastically reforming his father's organization, Warith Deen Muhammad aimed to bring the WCIW closer to the philosophy of traditional Islam, while strengthening its commitment to African Americans.

estate by the Messenger's heirs. And lastly, he decreed that the new Nation would continue to recognize Wallace Fard as Allah and Elijah Muhammad as Allah's Messenger.

Not surprisingly, Wallace Muhammad and Louis Farrakhan each declared himself the legitimate "spiritual heir" to Elijah Muhammad, and each claimed to have received the endorsement of the Messenger himself. To confirm the validity of the new Nation of Islam and to prove that Wallace had deviated from the true way, Farrakhan cited his 1972 conversation with Elijah Muhammad: "[T]he Nation is going to take a dive for the second time," the Messenger supposedly told him. "But, don't worry, brother. It will be rebuilt and it will never fall again. . . . Go exactly as you see me go and do exactly as you see me do . . . you must practice righteousness or [the enemy] will piece you in two."

Wallace also maintained that the Messenger fully approved of his preaching and had marked him as his successor from an early age. After he had been reinstated in the Nation in 1974, Wallace said, "I was free to propagate and preach as my own wisdom dictated. . . . I would say things I knew were different from [what] people had been taught under the leadership of Elijah Muhammad. . . . He never called me in and said what I was teaching was causing problems [or to] slow up or go in another direction."

A few weeks after the schism—mindful of the tragic outcome of Malcolm X's break with the movement and anxious to avoid further factionalism—Wallace urged his followers to refrain from protesting Farrakhan's meetings and from confronting the minister publicly. He even offered to restore to Farrakhan the ministry of the Harlem temple (Farrakhan declined the offer). For his part, Farrakhan made no attempt to divert members from the WCIW. While Wallace sought to transform the former Nation into a predominantly religious organization, Farrakhan believed it essential to reestablish the social force of the original Nation of Islam. Thus, although tumultuous at times, the schism was free of the violence of previous decades.

On September 10, 1978, Wallace—who was then known as Warith Deen Muhammad—resigned as leader of the WCIW, declaring that the Muslim community would thenceforth be led by a council of six *imams*, or directors, to be elected by democratic process. Warith would travel as an ambassador to the community, fulfilling an "evangelistic mission." The World Community of al-Islam in the West became the American Muslim Mission. By 1985, Warith had decentralized the movement completely, and the *Bilalian News*, which had been renamed the *American Muslim Journal*, was simply the *Muslim Journal*.

The American Muslim Mission has quietly prospered in the years following Warith's reforms. It has strengthened ties to the African-American community—while stressing the importance of unity among all races—by continuing to work to improve the housing and social conditions of urban dwellers. It has successfully developed an independent food-service industry, Salaam International. Though the American Muslims no longer actively pursue economic gains, they retain a number of properties and are financially sound. Through involvement with voter-registration programs and support of various political candidates, the organization has maintained a policy of political involvement whose foundation is religious faith.

But it is the renewed Nation of Islam that has captured the country's attention in recent years. During the first eight years of the new organization's existence, Louis Farrakhan traveled across the country establishing study groups that eventually became full-fledged temple communities. Although early followers included some dissatisfied members of the WCIW, most converts were new to the Nation of Islam or had been inactive members of the old Nation. The first Savior's Day celebration in 1981 was attended by 6,000 to 7,000 members.

Because Black Muslims traditionally distanced themselves from direct political involvement, they did not take part in the electoral process. In fact, one of the most radical changes Wallace Muhammad initiated was his voter-registration program. But in 1984, a presidential election year, African Americans had reached a milestone: for the first time in the country's history, a black man—Jesse Jackson—was campaigning for the presidency of the United States.

Jackson had served as an aide to Martin Luther King, Jr., from 1966 to 1968. He was applauded for his program to encourage academic excellence among ghetto youths, which he had established during the 1970s. Though, in 1972, New York Representative Shirley Chisholm had become the first African American to seek a presidential nomination, Jackson's presidential campaign marked a turning point. Many African-American leaders endorsed the Democrat's idea to create a "people's platform" for blacks and other minorities, a political alliance that would cross racial lines but would focus on the economic and social needs of African Americans. He forged an organization called the National Rainbow Coalition, Inc., which sponsored increased voter registration for blacks as a means to establish an African-American power base. Finally, the dream of equal involvement in national politics seemed possible for blacks.

Among those swept up in the excitement was Louis Farrakhan, who announced that he would register to vote for the first time. He publicly endorsed Jackson's candidacy and drew over 1,000 citizens to Chicago's City Hall in a mass registration of African-American voters.

Jesse Jackson was drawing large crowds of supporters and substantial media coverage when, early in 1984, he made a serious political mistake. In an aside not meant to be heard publicly, Jackson referred to Jews, in derogatory terms, as "Hymies," and to New York City as "Hymietown." A reporter for the *Washington Post*, Milton Coleman, heard the disparaging remarks and felt compelled to publish them. The February 3 article provoked a tremendous outcry against Jackson. Already under fire for his stormy relationship with Jews, Jackson first denied having made the statement and then apologized. But it was too late; his callous comments severely hobbled his campaign.

Farrakhan's 1985 tour to promote his plan for the economic development of black America was overshadowed by his inflammatory comments about Jews and his alleged link to the white supremacist Thomas Metzger. Here, Farrakhan makes his final tour appearance in Madison Square Garden, surrounded by female Fruit of Islam members known as the Vanguard. He was denounced by New York Mayor Ed Koch and Governor Mario Cuomo, and the Jewish Defense League held a "Death to Farrakhan" march outside the building.

Farrakhan's attempts to support Jackson only worsened the situation. Farrakhan assailed and threatened Jewish leaders who condemned Jackson, and he attacked Coleman, the African-American reporter who had recorded the comments, as a "no-good filthy traitor." Not only did Farrakhan's inflammatory remarks further jeopardize Jackson's campaign; they also cast an unfavorable light on the Nation of Islam, whose history with Jews had been even more turbulent than Jackson's.

Elijah Muhammad had spoken admiringly of American Jews. Perhaps because of his own efforts to secure economic and ethnic self-sufficiency for African Americans, he praised their business skills and sympathized with the Jewish history of religious persecution. But he was also fiercely critical and suspicious of them, for he believed that American Jews' support of Israel "against our [Muslim] brothers in the East" made them enemies. Moreover, Jews could not be the "chosen people" as they proclaimed, because the white man in Muhammad's theology was "the devil," and blacks were members of the original, chosen race.

Farrakhan continued Muhammad's practice of raging against Jews. After Jackson's unfortunate comment, Farrakhan claimed that "Israeli hit squads" were planning to kill Jackson. Soon after, Farrakhan responded to outraged protests against his words by comparing himself to a "very great man"—dictator Adolf Hitler—who also sought to "rais[e his] people up from nothing." Jesse Jackson himself eventually criticized Farrakhan, calling his remarks about Jews and about Hitler "unconscionable and reprehensible."

Although Jackson failed to win the Democratic nomination for president, his campaign, like that of Shirley Chisholm 12 years earlier, helped to shatter one of the last racial barriers that had kept African Americans from fully participating in national politics.

Soon after, the Nation came under fire again, when Thomas Metzger, head of a white supremacist group called the White American Political Association and a former Ku Klux Klan leader, claimed to have held a number of meetings with Farrakhan. The alleged affiliation caused an even greater scandal when Metzger unveiled a scheme to divide the continental United States into "whites-only" and "blacks-only" territories (other Americans, including Jews, would be restricted to small, "leftover" strips of land)—with control of the black territory going to the Nation of Islam. Although a spokesman for the Nation confirmed that Metzger had made a small donation to their movement, he denied that any meetings had taken place.

In 1985, Farrakhan embarked on a nationwide tour to promote a new strategy for the economic development of black America. Like the business enterprises of Elijah Muhammad during the 1950s and 1960s, People Organized and Working for Economic Rebirth (POWER) was designed to establish an economically independent African-American population in the United States by forging black-owned and black-run businesses. Although the 15-city tour drew little media attention, the concept of African-American economic autonomy appealed not only to members of the Nation but to the thousands of nonmembers who attended the rallies. The negative publicity the Nation had drawn the previous year threatened to overshadow Farrakhan's entire tour when, during his final appearance in New York, he was denounced by New York governor Mario Cuomo and Mayor Ed Koch and by the Jewish Defense League. Although over 25,000 people filled Madison Square Garden to hear Farrakhan speak, POWER itself eventually became a victim of the controversy, when the manufacturer of its proposed product line, a collection of cosmetics for African-American women, canceled its contract with the Nation.

Despite these problems, Farrakhan felt that his ministry was a success. Finally, he said, he had achieved Elijah Muhammad's goal of delivering the Nation's message to the whole country. In 1986, he declared that his evangelical period had come to an end. The time to establish a stable and solid ministry was at hand.

To this end, Farrakhan initiated changes in the Nation's practice of Islam. He placed increased emphasis on prayer and developed a program called "Self-Improvement: The Basis for Community Development," designed to encourage study of the Quran. Seeking to identify the Nation of Islam as part of a global struggle for human rights, he set off on an extensive trip through the Middle East in an effort to develop closer ties with Orthodox Islamic communities. In 1986, defying an executive order by President Ronald Reagan forbidding Americans

to visit Libya, Farrakhan met with the country's leader, Muammar El-Qaddafi, a longtime financial supporter of the Black Muslims. Upon his return to the United States, Farrakhan renewed his commitment to black economic progress. He revived his POWER program by unveiling the first six products in a black-oriented cosmetic line called "Clean and Fresh"—contracted to a different manufacturer and financed by a five-million-dollar loan from El-Qaddafi. It was the start of a new era in the Nation's effort to realize African-American financial independence.

But he did not stop there. In December 1994, Farrakhan called for African-American men to gather in a massive assembly before the Capitol Building in Washington, D.C. The Million Man March would demonstrate to the country the black man's renewed commitment to himself and to his community and would ensure that African-American men

In November 1993, members of the Nation of Islam join reporters to listen to Farrakhan's videotaped announcement of his plan for a week-long "Stop the Killing" rally in New York City. Farrakhan had been scheduled to speak at Yankee Stadium before the mayoral election that year, but his appearance was canceled for political reasons.

Young members of the Nation of Islam prepare for a Savior's Day assembly. During the Million Man March, Farrakhan petitioned African-American youths in particular to commit themselves to self-improvement and self-respect.

would "never again be looked at as the criminals, the clowns, the buffoons, the dregs of society."

On October 16, 1995, the country witnessed the largest gathering of African-American men in its history. Led by Farrakhan, a vast crowd of black men—doctors, auto mechanics, politicians, plumbers, athletes, truck drivers, students, attorneys, ministers, artists, entertainers, civil workers, businessmen—converged on the nation's capital for a day of spiritual renewal. Thousands of photographers and reporters gathered to record the event. Numerous black ministers and community leaders attended, in a rare show of solidarity with Farrakhan, to help celebrate the dignity and pride of African Americans.

"There's still two Americas—one black, one white, separated and unequal," Farrakhan proclaimed. He continued,

> We, as a people, who have been fractured, divided, and destroyed because of our division, now must move toward a perfect union. . . . We cannot continue the destruction of our lives and the destruction of our community. But the change can't come until we feel sorry. . . . [P]ointing out fault, pointing out

wrongs is the first step. The second step is to acknowledge [our guilt]. . . .

And so we stand here today at this historic moment; we are standing in the place of those who could not make it here today. We are standing in the blood of our ancestors. We are standing in the blood of those who . . . died in the fields and swamps of America, who died hanging from trees in the South . . . who died on the highways and in the fratricidal conflict that rages within our community. We are standing on the sacrifice of the lives of those heroes, our great men and women, that we today may accept responsibility that life imposes on each traveler who comes this way. . . . Now, brothers, moral and spiritual renewal is a necessity.

With his emphasis on African-American renewal and pride, Farrakhan harked back to the beginnings of the Black Muslim philosophy. The Nation of Islam arose during a time of social and economic upheaval in America, when African Americans—many of whom lacked education and training and were relegated to low-paying, low-status jobs—sought ways to overcome their difficulties and find a meaningful explanation for, and relief from, their condition. Like Marcus Garvey's UNIA and Noble Drew Ali's Moorish Temple of America, the Nation of Islam inspired hope in African Americans by providing a proud history of a noble race reaching back thousands of years.

Today, Louis Farrakhan's declarations, like the words of Elijah Muhammad and Malcolm X before him, continue to fire the imaginations of many African Americans. His remarks against nonblacks and his talk of a "final battle" between good and evil—that is, blacks and whites—may upset many people. Yet his blunt proclamations still ring true—most especially for the many Black Muslims who recognize that the reforms of the last few decades have failed to improve significantly the political and economic conditions of African Americans.

CHRONOLOGY

1897   Elijah Muhammad born Elijah Poole on October 7 in Bolds Springs, Georgia

1910   Thousands of blacks begin leaving the South to seek jobs in the industrial North
Black scholar W.E.B. Du Bois cofounds the National Association for the Advancement of Colored People (NAACP) and edits its journal, the *Crisis*

1915   Noble Drew Ali establishes the Moorish Temple of America

1917   The United States enters World War I; more than 360,000 blacks enlist and 42,000 see combat
Marcus Garvey establishes the UNIA in New York

1918   The return of thousands of soldiers at the end of World War I greatly increases the number of job seekers in America and intensifies racial tension across the country

1919   During the "Red Summer," race riots break out in over two dozen U.S. cities. Over 60 blacks are lynched

1920   The International Convention of the Negro Peoples of the World, a month-long display of black solidarity organized by Garvey, opens in New York City

1923   Garvey is convicted of mail fraud and sentenced to five years in prison
Elijah Poole moves his family to Detroit and joins the UNIA

1925   Malcolm X born Malcolm Little in Omaha, Nebraska, on May 19

1927   Garvey's prison sentence is commuted; he is deported to his native Jamaica

1929   The New York Stock Exchange crash on October 29 causes millions of Americans to lose their jobs
Noble Drew Ali implicated in philanthropist Julius Rosenwald's murder; dies soon after from unknown cause

1930   Elijah Poole meets Wallace Fard, founder of the Nation of Islam

1931   Poole joins the Nation of Islam and changes his name to Elijah Muhammad
Malcolm Little's father, Earl, a UNIA official, is murdered in East Lansing, Michigan

1933	Having been arrested three times, Fard is ordered to leave Detroit; he travels to Chicago
	Fard appoints Elijah Muhammad chief minister of the Nation of Islam and head of Temple Number One in Detroit
	Muhammad and teachers of the Nation's University of Islam are arrested; Muhammad moves the Nation's headquarters to Chicago after their release
	Louis Farrakhan born Louis Eugene Walcott in New York City on May 11
1934	Fard disappears mysteriously; Muhammad founds the Allah Temple of Islam, a faction of the Nation of Islam
1935	Muhammad flees rival factions in Chicago; begins traveling across the country, spreading Black Muslim teachings
1940	Malcolm Little moves to Boston to live with his half-sister, Ella
1941	Muhammad returns to Chicago; the Allah Temple of Islam becomes the Nation of Islam
	The FBI begins monitoring the Nation of Islam after a cache of weapons is discovered in Chicago headquarters
	The United States enters World War II
1942	Malcolm Little moves to Harlem; becomes a street hustler
	Muhammad arrested for refusing to register for the draft; sentenced to five years in the Federal Correction Institution in Michigan
1945	Malcolm Little arrested for robbery and sentenced to 10 years in the Charlestown State Prison in Massachusetts
1946	Muhammad is released from prison; returns to Chicago to assume leadership of the Nation of Islam
1949	Malcolm Little converts to the Nation of Islam while in prison; changes his name to Malcolm X
1952	Malcolm X earns early release from prison
1953	Malcolm X appointed minister for the Nation of Islam; organizes his first temple in Boston, Massachusetts

1954   Malcolm X appointed minister of Temple Number Seven in New York City

1955   Gene Walcott converts to the Nation of Islam; becomes Louis X

1957   Louis X named captain of the Fruit of Islam; appointed minister of Boston temple

1959   "The Hate That Hate Produced," a documentary on the Nation of Islam, airs on national television

1961   Malcolm X founds *Muhammad Speaks*, the newspaper of the Nation of Islam

1962   Malcolm X appointed national minister of the Nation of Islam
Muhammad, suffering from asthma and bronchitis, moves to Phoenix, Arizona
Black Muslims clash with police in Los Angeles; one member is killed, 12 are wounded

1963   Two former secretaries of Elijah Muhammad file paternity suits against him; rift between Muhammad and Malcolm X grows
250,000 people participate in the March on Washington for Jobs and Freedom on August 28; Malcolm X labels the peaceful demonstration a "Farce on Washington"
President John F. Kennedy is assassinated on November 22; Malcolm X is suspended from duties for 90 days for commenting on the event

1964   Malcolm X charged by Elijah Muhammad with plotting a rebellion; Muhammad excommunicates his son, Wallace, for complicity
Malcolm X breaks with the Nation of Islam on March 8; establishes Muslim Mosque, Incorporated; makes a religious pilgrimage to the Middle East; founds the Organization of Afro-American Unity; converts to Orthodox Islam and changes his name to El Hajj Malik El-Shabazz

1965   Malcolm X is assassinated in New York City on February 21
Wallace Muhammad is readmitted into the Nation of Islam

1971   Raymond Sharrief, Muhammad's son-in-law and bodyguard, is shot; members of a dissident Black Muslim group are murdered in retaliation; a guard of the Nation's Salaam Restaurant in Chicago is murdered

1972	Black Muslims are implicated in a street battle in Baton Rouge, Louisiana, which leaves four people dead
1973	Seven Hanafi Muslims are murdered in Washington, D.C.; Philadelphia Nation of Islam members are convicted of the crimes
	Hakim Jamal, head of the Malcolm X Foundation, is murdered; authorities believe the Nation of Islam is responsible
	James Shabazz, minister of the Newark temple, is killed; 11 members of a dissident group within the temple are convicted
1975	Muhammad dies on February 25; Wallace Muhammad is named his successor
	Wallace Muhammad removes Louis Farrakhan from his New York ministry
1976	The Nation of Islam becomes the World Community of al-Islam in the West (WCIW)
1978	Louis Farrakhan announces his departure from the WCIW on March 7; reestablishes the Nation of Islam
1984	Jesse Jackson campaigns for president of the United States; Farrakhan endorses him
1985	Farrakhan unveils his POWER program; tours the country promoting black-owned and black-run businesses; POWER product manufacturer cancels contract with the Nation
1986	Farrakhan meets with Libyan leader Muammar El-Qaddafi to obtain financing for the Nation of Islam
1987	Farrakhan renews his POWER program under new manufacturer
1995	Farrakhan leads Million Man March in Washington, D.C. on October 16

FURTHER READING

Cone, James H. *Martin & Malcolm & America: A Dream or a Nightmare?* New York: Orbis Books, 1991.

Cottman, Michael H. *Million Man March*. New York: Crown Publishers, Inc., 1995.

Halasa, Malu. *Elijah Muhammad: Religious Leader*. New York: Chelsea House, 1990.

Jakoubek, Robert. *Martin Luther King, Jr.: Civil Rights Leader*. New York: Chelsea House, 1989.

Lawler, Mary. *Marcus Garvey: Black Nationalist Leader*. New York: Chelsea House, 1988.

Lee, Martha F. *The Nation of Islam: An American Millenarian Movement*. New York: Syracuse University Press, 1996.

Magida, Arthur J. *Prophet of Rage: A Life of Louis Farrakhan and His Nation*. New York: HarperCollins Publishers, 1996.

Malcolm X and Alex Haley. *The Autobiography of Malcolm X*. New York: Grove Press, 1965.

Muhammad, Elijah. *Message to the Blackman in America*. Philadelphia: Hakim's Publications, 1965.

Rummel, Jack. *Malcolm X: Militant Black Leader*. New York: Chelsea House, 1989.

Weisbrot, Robert. *Freedom Bound: A History of America's Civil Rights Movement*. New York: Penguin Books USA, Inc., 1991.

WILLIAM H. BANKS, Jr., is co-author (with Arthur Hamilton) of the nonfiction book *Father Behind Bars*. He teaches creative writing at The New School for Social Research and Marymount Manhattan College in New York.

PICTURE CREDITS

page

2	AP/Wide World Photos		Research in Black Culture,	74-75	UPI/Bettmann
8	AP/Wide World Photos		New York Public Library,	77	UPI/Bettmann
13	AP/Wide World Photos		Astor, Tilden & Lenox	79	UPI/Bettmann
15	AP/Wide World Photos		Foundations	82	UPI/Bettmann Newsphotos
16-17	Corbis-Bettmann	50	The Bettmann Archive	86	AP/Wide World Photos
19	The Bettmann Archive	53	The Bostonian Society	88	AP/Wide World Photos
21	UPI/Bettmann	54	The Bettmann Archive	91	UPI/Bettmann Newsphotos
24	UPI/Bettmann	58	Schomburg Center for	95	UPI/Bettmann
27	UPI/Bettmann		Research in Black Culture,	98	AP/Wide World Photos
29	UPI/Bettmann		New York Public Library,	101	AP/Wide World Photos
34	Schomburg Center for		Astor, Tilden & Lenox	103	UPI/Corbis-Bettmann
	Research in Black Culture,		Foundations, photo by	104	AP/Wide World Photos
	New York Public Library		Austin Hansen	106	UPI/Bettmann
37	AP/Wide World Photos	61	UPI/Bettmann Newsphotos	110	UPI/Bettmann Newsphotos
39	AP/Wide World Photos	62	AP/Wide World Photos	114	AP/Wide World Photos
42	AP/Wide World Photos	65	UPI/Bettmann	117	AP/Wide World Photos
45	UPI/Bettmann	68	UPI/Bettmann Newsphotos	118	AP/Wide World Photos
47	Schomburg Center for	70	AP/Wide World Photos		